The Case Against French Colonization

By Nguyen-Ai-Quoc (Ho Chi Minh)

Translated by Joshua Leinsdorf

[Translator's note: Ho Chi Minh wrote in French which was a foreign language for him.]

Pentland Press

Copyright © 2017, by Joshua Leinsdorf

All rights reserved. No part of this publication may be reproduced, distributed, or transmitted in any form or by any means, including photocopying, recording, or other electronic or mechanical methods, without the prior written permission of the publisher, except in the case of brief quotations embodied in critical reviews and certain other noncommercial uses permitted by copyright law. For permission requests, write to the publisher, addressed "Attention: Permissions Coordinator," at the address below.

Pentland Press
60 Bayside Drive
Atlantic Highlands, NJ 07716

First Series

Colonial Mores

Worker's Library,
Quai de Jemmapes, 96,
Paris

Preface

In 1923, French colonization was the subject of a sensational trial.

The scandals in Togo and Cameroon caused such excitement among the natives subject to the French "mandate,"[1] that the League of Nations itself has ordered an investigation.

The case that we bring to court today includes the whole colonial domain belonging to French imperialism. We will, in turn, take the testimony of Senegalese, West Indians, Algerians, Tunisians, Malagasians, Annamese,[2] etc…, and the claims, as well as the complaints, of fifty-nine million colonial slaves, will be religiously collected in a series of pamphlets.

We start the series with the deposition of an Annamite: Nguyen-Ai-Quoc.

Another thing – it is not the humanitarian zeal of the League of Nations that is our concern, it is the Judgment of History we want to address. Thanks to our many, diverse, accurate and "living" documents, future humanity, to whom we wish a better life, can judge the colonial crusade at its true value.

Then, it is to the colonial people themselves that we appeal. The day, and that day is coming, when these masses, who have been, in effect, enslaved, regain their freedom, they will then establish a revolutionary Tribunal to try the colonial clique as it deserves.

We are told – but what about civilization?[3] It is true: French colonization brings the railroad, the electric tram, wireless telegraphy (not counting the Gospel and the Declaration of the Rights of Man); the questions are, who opens their wallets to pay for these wonders? Who sweats to build these machines? Who benefits from the welfare they bring? And who receives the dividends they yield? – Is it us, or those who exploit and oppress us? Is it the blacks of Sudan and the yellow of Annam, or the conquistadors with pink faces, stealing our land and our herds, and taking the fruits of our labor, after killing our countrymen?

France, or more precisely the French people, have repeatedly been used to undertake distant, costly, and bloody, conquests. They are prevailed upon to justify the unspeakable crimes that plague the colonies daily, but go unpunished. Do these people take the least profit from the colonial scramble, or are they exploited, like us, by the same exploiters?

Ng. The Truyen.

First Chapter

Blood Tax

I. War and the Natives

Before 1914, they were only niggers and dirty Annamese good at the very most for pushing rickshaws and receiving the blows of administrators. The joyous new war declared, they became "good friends" and "dear children" of our paternal and tender officials and even our more or less general governors.[4] They (the natives) were suddenly promoted to the rank of supreme "defenders of justice and freedom." This honor they suffered, however, cost them dearly, because to defend this justice and freedom of which they are deprived, they had to suddenly leave their rice fields or sheep, their children and wives, to cross the oceans and rot on the battlefields of Europe. During the crossing, many natives, after seeing a wonderful display of the scientific maneuver of torpedoing, went to the bottom of the waves to defend the homeland of the sea monsters. Others left their skin on the poetic desert of the Balkans wondering if the mother-country intended to be the first to enter the Turkish Harem, or else why were they being killed in this country? Others, on the banks of the Marne or mud of Champagne, were heroically massacred to sprinkle their blood on the leaders' laurels and sculpt the marshals' batons with their bones.

Finally, to not have to breathe the poison gas of the "Boches",[5] those who toiled in the rear in the monstrous gunpowder factories, submitted to the glowing French fumes; which amounted to the same thing since the poor devils spit out their lungs as if they had been gassed.

In all, 700,000 Vietnamese natives came to France, and of this number, 80,000 will never again see the sun in their country!

II. The Enlisted

A colleague told[6] us that all forms of taxes, interest, corvée labor of every kind, mandatory purchases of alcohol and opium, constantly squeeze the native proletariat of Indochina. Since 1915 – 16, they have also undergone the ordeal of being enlisted.

The events of these last years have provided grounds for great grabs of human material throughout the country and confined them to barracks under the most diverse names: infantryman, semi-skilled workers, unskilled workers, etc.

In the opinion of all impartial powers that were called upon to utilize the Asian human material in Europe, this material did not produce results commensurate with the huge expenses incurred by its transport and maintenance.

This hunting of said human material, called for the occasion "volunteers" (a word of frightful irony), then gave rise to the most scandalous abuses.

Here is how this voluntary recruitment is practiced: The "saytrap" that is each one of the Indochinese Résidents,[7] informs his mandarins that it is necessary that his Province supply a certain number of men by a fixed deadline. The means are unimportant. The mandarins manage. They are familiar with the coping mechanism, especially for monetizing this business.

They begin by gathering available subjects, who, without resources, are sacrificed without recourse. Then they summon the sons of the rich; if they are recalcitrant, an occasion is easily found to examine their history, or their family's, and, when necessary, imprison them until they have resolved the following dilemma: "enlist or pay."

It is conceivable that people picked up under such circumstances lack any enthusiasm for their intended profession. Just barely barracked, they watch for any opportunity to escape.

Others, unable to protect themselves from what is for them a bad fate, inoculate themselves with the most serious diseases, the most common is purulent conjunctivitis, from rubbing the eyes with various ingredients, ranging from lime to gonorrheal pus.

•
• •

Even so, having promised to give mandarin rank to Vietnamese volunteers who survived and posthumous titles to those who are dead "for the native land," the general government continued its proclamation: "You enlisted *in droves*: you riflemen, to give blood; you workers, to offer your arms; and left your homeland though to which you are so attached, *without hesitation*."

If the Annamites were so delighted to be soldiers, why were they taken to the capital in chains, while others awaited embarkation locked within the College of Saigon, under the eye of French sentinels with fixed bayonets and loaded guns? The bloody events in Cambodia, the riots in Saigon, Bien-Hoa and elsewhere, were they, therefore, manifestations of this eagerness to join up "in droves" and "without hesitation"?

The escapes and desertions (50 percent in the class of reservists) provoked ruthless repressions, and these revolts were suppressed in blood.

The General government took care to add that, of course, to merit the "visible benevolence" and the "great goodness" of the administration, "You (Indochinese soldiers) must conduct yourselves well and give no cause for dissatisfaction."

The senior commander of the troops in Indochina took another precaution; he had inscribed on the back or wrist of each recruit an indelible number made using a solution of silver nitrate.

As in Europe, the great misery of some is the cause of profit for others: commissioned officers, for who this windfall of recruitment and management of natives permits them to remain as long as possible away from perilous operations in Europe; suppliers who enrich themselves quickly by starving the unfortunate recruits; and black marketeers who have illicit dealings with officials.

Let us add, in this connection, there is another kind of volunteering, volunteering for subscriptions to various loans. Identical procedures. Whoever has the means is required to subscribe. Persuasive and coercive methods are used against the recalcitrants such that all subscribe.

As most Asian subscribers are ignorant of French financial mechanisms, they consider the payments to loans as new taxes and value the securities as receipts.

.
. .

Now see how volunteerism has been organized in the other colonies.

Take, for example, West Africa (now Senegal, Mauritania, Sudan, Upper Volta, Guinea, Niger, Ivory Coast and Dahomey):

Commanders, accompanied by their armed forces, went from village to village to force the Notable natives to provide IMMEDIATELY the number of men they wanted to recruit. Was a commander not considered ingenious to make young Senegalese who fled before him leave their hiding place and don the military Fez, by torturing their parents? Did he not stop the elderly, pregnant women, young girls, and make them strip off their clothes and burn them before their eyes? Naked and bound, under the blows of the cane, the unfortunate victims were run through the towns on the double "to set an example"! A woman carrying her baby on her back had to ask permission to have a free hand to balance her child. Two old men dropped from inanition during the journey; girls, terrorized by such cruelties, had their menstrual period for the first time; a pregnant woman gave birth prematurely to a stillborn child; another gave birth to a blind child.

∴

The processes of recruitment elsewhere were highly diverse. This one was particularly expeditious:

A string is stretched at the end of the main street of a village and another string at the other end. And all the Negroes found between the two strings are automatically volunteered.

"March 3, 1923, at noon," a witness wrote us, "the wharfs of Rufisque and Dakar having been ringed by the constabulary, all of the natives who worked there were rounded-up. As these fellows did not seem willing to go immediately to defend civilization, they were asked to get into trucks that led them to prison. From there, after they had taken the time to reconsider, they were taken to the barracks.

"There, following patriotic ceremonies, 29 volunteers to the last man were proclaimed potential heroes ... All now burning with desire to return the Ruhr to the mother-country.

"Only," wrote General Mangin, who knew them well, these are the troops "to consume before winter."

We have in hand a letter from a native of Dahomey, a veteran who has done his "duty" in the just war. Excerpts from this letter will show you how "batouala"[8] are protected and how our colonial administrators manufacture the native loyalty that dec-

8

orate all official speeches and feed all the articles by the Regismansets and Hausers.[9]

"In 1915," the letter said, "At the time of forced recruiting ordered by Mr. Noufflard, Governor of Dahomey, my village was pillaged and burned by police officers and the Circle[10] guards. During the looting and burning, all I had was taken from me. Nevertheless, I was enlisted by force, and in spite of this heinous attack of which I was the victim, I have done my duty at the French front. I was wounded at Aisne.

"Now that the war is over, I will return to my country, homeless and without resources.

"Here is what I was robbed of:
"1,000 francs in cash;
"12 pigs;
"15 sheep;
"10 goats;
"60 chickens;
"8 loin cloths;
"5 jackets;
"10 pants;
"7 headdresses;
"1 silver necklace;
"2 trunks containing various objects.

"Here are the names of comrades living in the same neighborhood as me who were enlisted by force, the same day as me, and whose houses were looted and burned. (Seven names follow.)

"Many are still the victims of Governor Noufflard's military exploits, but I do not know their names to give them to you today…."

The "Boches" of [Kaiser] Wilhelm could have done no better.

III. The Fruit of Sacrifice

As soon as the guns were sated with the black or yellow flesh, the romantic declarations of our leaders fell silent as if by magic and Negroes, and Annamites automatically changed back into people of the "dirty race."

In commemoration of services rendered, before embarking from Marseilles, were not the Annamites stripped of everything they had: new clothes purchased at their expense, watches, various souvenirs, etc…? Were they not subjected to the control of thugs who beat them for no reason? Were they not fed like pigs and laid as such in humid holds, without berths, airless, and without light? Having arrived in their country, were they not warmly received by the grateful administrator with this patriotic speech: "You have defended the homeland. This is good. Now, we no longer need you, go away!"

And the former "poilus"[11] – or what remains of them – after having valiantly defended law and justice, returned empty handed to their native status where law and justice are unknown.

∴

According to the Indochinese newspapers, opium vendor licenses would be granted to mutilated Frenchmen and to widows of the French soldiers killed in the war.

Thus, the colonial government committed two crimes against humanity at the same time. On one hand, it is not happy to do the dirty work of poisoner personally, it wants to involve the poor victims of fratricidal butchery. On the other hand, it values the life and blood of its dupes so low, that it believes that by throwing them these rotten bones; it is sufficient payment for dismemberment or mourning a husband.

We have no doubt that the cripples and widows of war will reject this repugnant offer by spitting their indignation in the face of its author. We are certain that the civilized world and the good French are with us in condemning the colonial sharks that do not hesitate to poison an entire people to fill their own pockets.

.
. .

Following the Annamite custom, if, in a village, someone died, the rice hullers must show respect for the repose of the soul of the deceased and the grief of his family by refraining from singing, as they normally do, during their work. Modern civilization, implanted by force among us, is different. Read the following story that was published in a Cochinchinese newspaper:

Celebrations of Bien Hoa

"The committee to organize the celebrations for the benefit of the *monument to the dead* Annamites from Bien Hoa Province is actively working to put together a wonderful program.

"We are talking about a *garden-party*, fairgrounds, a *country dance*, etc…., in short, the *attractions are many and varied* to allow everyone to collaborate on a good work in *the most pleasant way* in the world.

"Gentlemen aviators of Bien Hoa air base will lend their aid and organizers can already count on the presence of the highest Saigonese authorities to boost the radiance of the festival.

"Let us add that the Saigonese men and women will not need to return to the capital for dinner, which would thus cut short *their cakewalk. A beautifully prepared, specially garnished buffet will satisfy the most discerning palates.*

"Let's all go to Bien Hoa January 21st. There will be *lovely celebrations,* and we will have shown the families of Bien Hoa's Annamites who died during the war that we know how to remember their sacrifice."

Other times, other manners.

But what manners!

The following letter was sent to us:

Saigon

"…It is a painful and grotesque anomaly to celebrate the victory of 'law' and 'justice' to people who both suffer injustice and have no rights. This is exactly what has been done here. It is unnecessary to tell you about the festivities and 'public pleasures' that took place in this city on November 11th. It is always the same everywhere: torchlight parades, fireworks, review the troops, a ball at the Governor's Palace, flower parade, patriotic collections, advertisements, speeches, banquets, etc. Of all these hypocrisies, I have retained only one psychologically interesting fact. Like the crowds of all countries, those of Saigon are very fond of movies. Thus, a dense mass camped in front of the Charlot and Palace Theaters where films run continuously and glorious cowboys march by one after the other. The crowd took over the street, invading the boulevard. Then the owner of the Saigon-Palace, wanting to unblock the sidewalk in front of his establishment, hit the crowd with a rattan cane. Madame also helped and beat the multitude. A few newsboys succeeded in 'pinching' the cane of the missus; and we applauded. Enraged, the proprietor returned to the contest, this time with a club, and he struck, heroically, with a vengeance. The 'peasants'[12] were pushed back to the boulevard, but drunk with his 'victory', this good Frenchman bravely crossed the street and continued to rain his big cane on the head, shoulders, and backs of these poor natives. A child was taken by him and generously 'bastinadoed'….

IV. THE CONTINUOUS MILITARISM

Upon his arrival in Casablanca, Field Marshal Lyautey sends the troops of the Moroccan occupation army the order for the next day:

"I owe you the highest military merit with which I have been honored by the Republican government because, for nine years, you gave unstinting dedication and *your blood*.

"We will launch a campaign that will ensure the final pacification of Morocco for the *common benefit of its loyal populations* and of the protectress nation, etc."

Yet, on the same day (the 14th of April) comes this press release:

"During an engagement with the Beni-Bou-Zert at Bab-el-Harba we had 29 killed and 11 injured."

When you think that it took the blood of one million five hundred thousand workers to manufacture six marshals' batons, the 29 poor bastards who died is not enough applause for the eloquent speeches of the résident Field Marshal. But where is the right of peoples to self-determination, for which we killed each other for four years? And what a funny way to civilize: to teach people to live well, by killing them.

. . .

Here (in Haiphong), there are also seamen's strikes. Thus Thursday (August15) two ships had to leave taking a large number of Annamite infantrymen *to Syria.*

The sailors refused to leave, claiming that their wages were not being paid in piasters. In fact, the piaster's market value was 10 francs instead of the official rate of 2.5. The companies established an unheard of abuse, the sailors' rate was in francs while the officials were paid in piasters.

Everyone was then disembarked and the men of the crew were immediately arrested.

As you can see, sailors in the Yellow Sea have nothing to envy of the Black Sea sailors.[13]

We protest with all our strength against sending Annamite troops to Syria. Is it believed, in high places, that not enough of our unfortunate yellow brothers were massacred on the battlefields between 1914 and 1918, during the "war for civilization and justice?"

.
. .

It is customary among our glorious ones "to educate" the natives with kicks and caning.

The unfortunate Nahon was twice murdered, first by Captain Vidart, and then by the avaricious quack in charge of the autopsy, who, to save his buddies' skins, did not hesitate to steal and hide the brain of the deceased – he is not, unfortunately, the only victim of colonial militarism. One of our colonial colleagues reported another:

"This time," he said, "It was at the headquarters of the 5th Infantry. The victim was a young soldier of the 21st class, Terrier, a native of Ténès. [Algeria]

"The circumstances of his death are particularly painful. On August 5, the young soldier Terrier went to the regimental infirmary to ask for a purgative. He was given, or more precisely what he believed to be, the purgative; he drank it, and a few hours later, writhing in agony, he died.

"Mr. Terrier's father then received a telegram telling him, bluntly without explanation, his son, - his only son, - had died and that he will be buried next day, Sunday.

"Mad with grief, the poor father runs to Algiers, to the 5th Infantry headquarters. There he learns that the body of his son is in the Maillot hospital. (How was he carried there? Is it true that to avoid the regulatory verification required for all deaths occurring in the infirmary, he was taken *dead* to the hospital, under the pretense of having died on the way?)

"In the hospital, the unfortunate father asks to see the corpse, *he is told to wait.*

"Long after, a Major arrives who tells him that the autopsy just done *revealed nothing* and leaves *without giving him permission to see the body of his son.*

"The latest news - it seems that Mr. Terrier, the father, who asked for an explanation from the 5th Infantry Colonel, has received this response: *his son died drunk.*'

CHAPTER II

Poisoning of Natives

Good Mr. Sarraut, former radical[14] Minister of Colonies, little father of the natives (as he says), adored the Annamites and was adored by them.

To inculcate the French civilization of which he was the principal agent, he stopped at nothing, not even disgraceful acts and crimes. Here is the proof: In the letter in his capacity as Governor General of Indochina, to fatten the pockets of the colonial bandits and his own, he addresses his subordinates:

"Mr. Résident,

"By order of the Director General of Management, I have the honor to request you to kindly support the efforts of my service in the establishment of new places for the consumption of opium and alcohol.

"To this effect, let me send you *a list of establishments it would be necessary to install* in the various villages mentioned, most of which are totally without alcohol and opium.

"Using the Cambodian governors and Messocks[15] your preponderant influence could well emphasize, to some small indigenous merchants, the benefits they would have by engaging in additional trading.

"As for our part, the operational field service agents, on their rounds, will pick the locations, unless you prefer, Mr. Résident, for them to wait for you to act first with the authorities and then support your action, in which case I ask you kindly to inform me.

"It is only by a full and consistent agreement between your administration and ours that we will get our best result, for the greater good of the interests of the revenue."

Signed, Albert Sarraut

There were then 1500 vendors of alcohol and opium per 1000 villages while there were only ten schools for the same number of localities. Already, before this famous letter, 12 million natives – including women and children – were downing 23 – 24 million liters of alcohol per year.

"For the monopolies, Indochina will be represented by a beautiful deer, mercilessly bound, dying under the crooked beak of insatiable vultures."

The company of the alcohol monopoly counted among its underwriters the most eminent figures of Indochina and all branches of the Administration there were brilliantly represented. Most of them had the advantage of being undeniably useful;

Justice, to settle disputes with those we want to tax:

2 attorneys general;
1 prosecutor of the Republic;
1 notary clerk.

The army, to repress a revolt that is considered possible only because of the monopoly:

1 brigadier general;
1 lieutenant colonel;
2 high grade military doctors;
1 commander;
2 captains.

The administration, whose disinterested complacency would be the best guarantee for the success of the operation:

1 résident of France;
1 recipient of finances;
1 paymaster general;
1 postal inspector;
1 registrar;
1 director of civil services;
2 teachers, etc., etc.

Finally: The Honorable Mr. Clementel, Member of Parliament from Puy-de-Dôme.

. .
.

"What France sees and is proud of!" cried Mr. Sarraut at the Colonial Exposition in Marseille. In fact, here beside the majestic alligators of West Africa, camels from Tunis yawn philosophically, and the friendly Malagache crocodiles gossip familiarly with august Indochinese cows. Agreement was never so perfect, and facing the peaceful invasion of colonial fauna, the legendary sardine[16] of the old port, a good hostess, smiles graciously.

The visitors view with lively interest the historical sofa of a Governor General, the sword with which administrator résident Darles pricked the thighs of Tonkinese inmates, and the torch that the administrator Bruère used to smoke out more than 200 natives from Housassas.

The flag of Cameroon especially attracts attention. We see a board bearing these patriotic words:
"Germans in Cameroon imported 'large quantities of alcohol.'
"The French have banned its use."

However, a malicious hand sticks to the bottom of this board the letter of Mr. Sarraut requiring his subordinates to increase the number of alcohol and opium levies in the Annamite villages, with this inscription:
"When the Annamites already have: 10 schools, 1,500 alcohol and opium outlets for 1,000 villages."

. . .

A significant fact about an official who was the head of Son-Tay province in Tonkin.

In this province, there was a population estimated at 200,000 inhabitants. For the cause, when it came to pushing consumption, this population rose with a sudden rapidity: it was increased to 230,000 inhabitants. But, as these 230,000 inhabitants consumed too little, the Résident of Son-Tay arrived, after a year, to obtain a consumption of 560,000 liters of alcohol.

Right away, his promotion was ensured; he received congratulations.

Mr. C... affirms that another Résident showed him a letter from further up the chain of command in which it says: "The alcohol consumed in Prefecture X... has fallen to less than Z..., per capita. Don't you think it is necessary to make an example? The Résident summons the notables and put them on notice, explaining to them that if they were consuming so little, that they must be smuggling; and soon villages, for the sake of peace, bought the imposed amount of alcohol, proportionate to the number of officially estimated inhabitants.

It is fixed, in fact if not by legal means, the annual consumption of each native. And when we say *each native*, we must not forget that it is not only adult natives; it is the *entire population*; it is old men, women, children, even those at the breast; the parents are forced in some way to substitute for them to consume not one, but two, or three liters of alcohol.

The inhabitants of a Tonkin village, forced to consume, seeing the threat to themselves, addressed themselves to their European official:

"We do not even have enough to eat." The officer replied: "You are accustomed to three meals of rice a day; You just have to eliminate one meal, or, if necessary, a meal and a half to consume the government alcohol."

Hitherto, the natives were accustomed to purchasing alcohol in small quantities, and they could take delivery in vessels that suited them. But now the system of stamped bottles has been established. Alcohol can be delivered only in official bottles of half-liters or liters. The Annamites were used to an alcoholic content of 20 to 22 percent; alcohol of 40 to 45 percent is imposed on them. They were accustomed to drink alcohol that had a pleasant empyreumatical[17] taste, due to the quality of the raw materials they employed, including a more delicate rice: the drug Annamites are forced to swallow is made with cheap rice, chemical ingredients and has a dirty taste.

The monopolists brought out a circular to stipulate to their employees the dilution of alcohol to be sold: to a hectoliter of alcohol, it was to mix 8 liters of pure water.

We have calculated that, given that each day 500 hectoliters of this alcohol is sold in Indochina, including 4,000 liters of clean water, and that 4,000 liters at 30 cents per day makes 1,200 piasters per day, 36,000 piasters per month, a small profit from only one spring of 432,000 piasters or 4 million francs per year!

Thus alcohol, such as is manufactured and sold by the monopolists of Indochina, does not match in strength or taste what the natives desire, and must be pushed on them by force.

The administration is pressed by the constant need for money. The requirement to meet the increasing expenses of colonial government, large loans, military construction and the need to find – if not real jobs – at least salaries for a host of officials imposed upon it by Paris; pushes administration officials and agents, from the Résident to the humblest employee, to increase, by hook or by crook, the consumption of alcohol.

CHAPTER III

The Governors

I. Mr. Fourn

Mr. Fourn, Governor of Dahomey, governs so well that all the natives of the colony complain about him. To calm the discontent, authorities pretend to send an inspector to the colony. This one inspects so well that he fled[18] the camp without considering the complaints presented to him by the population.

We have received, on this subject, a letter from the Franco-Muslim Action Committee in Porto-Novo. Here are the essential passages:

"Well before the arrival of the French in Dahomey, there was in Porto-Novo a Muslim leader called Imam, responsible for representing the Moslem community wherever necessary, administering the property belonging to this community and ensuring the celebration of religious ceremonies.

"According to custom, the Imam must be elected by an electoral body of devout Muslims noted for their morality and who have filled the assistant positions over a long period. Furthermore, before his death, the Imam in power gives his opinion on the deputy who, currently, possesses the qualifications required to replace him.

"The opinion given by the Imam on this occasion is irreversible.

"Before the death of the Imam Cassoumou, the latter named as his successor the deputy Saroukou, who was accepted by the electoral body as well as the majority of Moslems.

"The Imam Saroukou should have been elected upon the death of Cassoumou, but Ignacio Paraiso, *with the backing of the Governor*, opposed it by arbitrarily imposing on the Moslems the appointed Lawani Kassoko, who is his personal friend and who, like him, is a Moslem in name only.

"Seeing that the electoral body and the majority of Moslems were against the illegal appointment of Lawani Kassoko, Mr. Ignacio Paraiso interposed the higher chief Houdji, who is a primitivist, and who *under the cover of government authority* elected the appointed Lawani Kassoko contrary to wishes of Muslims.

"Again, if Lawani Kossoko were a good and honest Moslem, we would keep silent about his appointment, but he is the most dishonest man on earth.

Here is more than enough evidence of what we say.

"Lawani Kassoko was born in Lagos (English Nigeria). He is a British subject. Following killings and other crimes committed in English Nigeria, Lawani Kassoko was pursued by the British authorities.

"*Our Governor then took in this undesirable British subject and, as a reward, appointed him chief of the lake villages*: Affotonou, Aguegue, Agblankantan, etc. etc., where now all the inhabitants have had enough of his exactions and crimes and complained about it.

"- We had a mosque in the Akpassa neighborhood in Porto-Novo. The French administration demolished this mosque for a public utility and gave us an indemnity of 5,000 francs.

"The compensation was not enough for the construction of a new mosque; we collected, by private subscription, a sum of 22,000 francs.

"Among the members of the Committee responsible for the purchase of materials and payment of workers, was Ignacio Paraiso.

"On the death of Imam Assistant Bissirou, who had been entrusted with the key to the safe, Ignacio Paraiso became the custodian of the key. He took advantage of this title to divert a total of 2,775 francs. The Committee was obliged to remove him.

"Ignacio Paraiso, irate, *consulted with the Governor. He took arbitrary measures against us and put obstacles in the way of constructing our mosque.*

"Now, as a result of the intrigues of Ignacio Paraiso, *to which the Governor lent a hand*, upon the naming of unholy Lawani Kassoko as Imam, the Moslems of Porto-Novo have been divided into two camps. This state of affairs undermines the harmony and free exercise of our religion, and has created great confusion."

II. Mr. Long

Excerpts from a letter to the June 12, 1922 edition of *French Republic* by Colonel Bernard who, you may rest assured Mr. Minister, is not a communist.

"The exports of Indochina," says the letter, "Are stationary or even falling. In 1914, Indochina exported: 45,000 kilos of silk; 99,000 tons of corn; 480 tons of tea; last year, it exported only 15,000 kilos of silk; 32,000 tons of corn and 156 tons of tea.

"It is also believed that the Indochinese government is now actively pursuing the execution of projects necessary for the development of the colony. Yet, since 1914, we have built neither *a kilometer of railroad track nor a hectare of rice paddy*. Ten years ago, Mr. Sarraut did approve a program of work that included construction of the railway from Vinh to Dong Ha, and the making of four large irrigation systems. All work has been suspended for more than five years, on the pretext that there was no financing available. Now, in this same period, Indochina has spent 65 million piasters and 450 million francs on road construction and civilian buildings. Let Mr. Faget[19] well contemplate these numbers! The expense of nearly half a billion to construct car roads that carry not a ton of goods and to raise housing and offices for staff who swarm in Indochina with the abundance of tropical vegetation; moreover, during that time, admittedly essential work, already approved by a vote of parliament, was abandoned.

"And do not think that we have any intention of changing methods in Indochina. To complete the program of 1912, Mr. Long has already asked parliament for permission to incur borrowing; he asks today for permission to take out a second loan. Those who lead the development of Indochina today seem determined not to do anything truly useful if you do not allow them, firstly, to make debts. As for the budgetary resources, as to reserves accumulated during the war and post-war period, they are determined to royally throw them out the window if parliament does not remedy the situation.

III. Mr. Garbit

Mr. Garbit, Governor General of Madagascar, returned to France. Like all the Governors, his friends, Mr. Garbit is very happy with "HIS" colony. Progress, wealth, loyalty, projects, calm, organization, etc., that is the eternal unchanging baggage of proconsuls on leave that Mr. Garbit, in his turn, unpacks obligingly for anyone to see. And, beyond these falsehoods, Mr. Garbit artfully tosses out another deception (or the deception of another) this superfine: development of colonies. In welcoming him, it is asked of Mr. Governor:

"Is it true that the inspection mission, sent by the ministry, did not have enough soap to wash the head of the Governor[20] and grease the slope on which his Excellency must slide toward the Metropole [France], there to remain forever and ever?

"Is it true, to save face, some zealous ones have organized a reception before his departure; and that this necessitated a laborious recruitment, because nobody, outside of the organizers, wanted to come?

"Is it true that the tools of Mister Governor had planned a petition asking his return to the colony; but that this petition did not see the light of day because it was thought to be a counter-petition?

"Is it true, finally, that the affectionate wish the indigenous population addressed to him was this:

"Goodbye, Garbit! Hope we never meet again!"

IV. Mr. Merlin

The fate of twenty million happy Annamese is placed in the hands of Mr. Martial Merlin.

"Who is this Mr. Merlin?" you ask me. This is a man who has been director of the Gambier Islands, then general secretary of West Africa, then Governor of the same colony. This is a man who has spent thirty-six years of his life stuffing indigenous skulls with the civilization of benefactress France.

Perhaps you would say it is an enormous indo-chinoiserie[21] to govern a country by a man who understands nothing about it.

Well! Yes. But it is the fashion. A colleague pointed out that enthroned in the Office of the Ministry of West Africa colonies, is a former director of Indochina. – A former administrator of West Africa is responsible for services in Equatorial Africa. – A past official of Sudan was chosen to address issues concerning Madagascar; while Cameroon is represented at the colonial exposition by an official who has never set foot there.

So, before going to civilize the Indochinese in Indochina, the proconsul Merlin wanted to start by civilizing the Indochinese dead in France, you know, these who died for their country, justice and *so on*.

Laughter in cemeteries is a pleasure of great men, but to laugh there all alone would probably be unseemly. That is why his Excellency Martial Merlin instructed the young state-supported Annamites to accompany him to the Garden of the Dead at Nogent-Sur-Marne for a speech to be made in his high presence. But, before being read to the public, said speech had to be presented to his Excellency for censorship. This was done, and the speech, judged too subversive, was canceled altogether by His Excellency and replaced by another, for which His Excellency himself gave the outline.

Naturally, the speech thus cooked in the official sauce smelled strongly of loyalty and unwavering commitment.

If the dead could speak, as the spiritualists

claim, the Annamite ghosts of Nogent would say, "Th...anks[22] *to you, oh Governor! But have mercy, - leave us in peace.*"

V. Mr. Jeremie Lemaire

We read in the *Colonial Annals* this tidbit:

"We learn that Jeremie La Maire, former colonial Governor, former Deputy of India, is currently the object of criminal prosecution. Indeed, he was President of the bank of which Mr. Frezouls was the managing director; a bank declared bankrupt two years ago.

"This is the culmination of the career of this sad individual."

Well, Well! So there are some sad individuals in the noble brotherhood of Governors and colonial Deputies? Who would have thought it!

VI. Mr. Outrey

He is a Cochinchinese Member of Parliament (as Cochinchinese as Mr. P. Loti[23] is Turkish). He makes speeches at the palace and does business in Saigon. As a parliamentarian, he regularly puts the touch on his seals of office; as a colonist, he does not pay his taxes. This honest representative of the people has a concession of 2,000 hectares, and, for fifteen years, the honorable concessionaire has not paid a cent. When the tax collector asked him to come into compliance, he replied: Th...ank you. Because he is a Member of Parliament, he is left alone.

There was a time when this same Mr. Outrey was interim Governor of Cochinchina.

Cochinchina is administered by a Governor appointed by decree of the President of the Republic. This *high* officer is helped in his *high* functions by a mixed Assembly, the Colonial Council, one of whose functions, the most important, no doubt, is to vote, every year, the budget of the colony. We must say at once that this budget is funded by revenue from taxes, either direct or indirect, *paid by the Annamites.* The expenditures therein provided for should be made, in principle (*but never in actuality!*) *for the Annamites.* In a word, *it is the Annamese interests* that are entrusted to this Colonial Council. At present, this famous Colonial Council is composed of more French than Annamese: 18 French members, including 12 elected and 6 delegates from different associations: the Chamber of Commerce, the Chamber of Agriculture, etc., and *6 Annamite members*. Assuming all are present, what can 6 Annamese voices do against 18 French votes? The government consequently puts into the budget whatever it pleases, and it is certain in advance that these items will be approved.

This is what happens three-quarters of the time: that is how, in 1905, the interim Governor Outrey, today a Deputy of France in Cochinchina, raised by *one hundred percent*, the already too heavy taxes that fall on the rice fields. This increase, that has immortalized Outrey in the memory of Annamites, resulted in the collective resignation of our indigenous Councilors. No matter! Outrey had them replaced by others he imposed himself on the Annamite voters.

One of his enforcement officers, the administrator Maspero (province of Bien Hoa), did he not lock in prison all voters in the province, on the eve of the election, to prevent them from communicating with the candidates? They were thus forced to vote, under penalty of reprisals, for Outrey's candidate Bùi-Thê-Kam, to prevent the re-election of resigned Councilor Hoài; who had refused to act as Outrey wanted.

CHAPTER IV

The Administrators

I. M. Saint

As you know, the colonies are Frances overseas, and the French of these Frances are the Annamites or the Malagasies, or the …etc. Also, that which is good here is bad there, and what is tolerated over there is forbidden here. For instance: It is permissible for all French to brutalize the native with opium, the more sold, the more they are esteemed, but if you dare to sell this poison here, you will immediately be put away. On the other hand, in France, a senior official is permitted to travel in underwear; contrariwise, it is prohibited for a native prince to wear native dress, even when he is sick at home.

Being sick, the incandescent Bey of Tunis received the Résident-General in a dressing gown. Now, this was bad enough, but worse was that the grandson and nephew of the same Bey had forgotten to greet the aforementioned Résident. Two days later, just at siesta time, Mr. Résident, in his smart uniform, escorted by his troops, came to demand an apology. It was done. When the Bey is under the protection of a saint, whether the Holy father, holy son or holy spirit, he has no right to be sick. And you "Poulbot"[24] natives know that when you are born under the wing of mother democracy, you must not play, or laugh, or heckle, but learn to greet.

In Indochina, and other colonies, many "guardians" are happy to beat the natives who do not salute fast enough: but they never called up the armed forces to ask greetings from their "toddlers" again. It is true that they are not all Résident-Generals.

Although this "serious event" was reported from the rostrum of parliament, it could, as M. Poincaré[25] said, injure the influence of France. We can not, without being ungrateful to the Résident-General Saint, accuse[26] him of "defeatism", because, thanks to this friendly, child-like and peaceful demonstration, the natives henceforth know how to greet a "white brother." We recall that during his visit to Africa, M. Millerand was welcomed by the natives who, to show their sincere affection and reverence to the protector head of state, pull their shirts out of their pants.

II. Mr. Darles

Notes On Human Rights[27] recently published a letter from M. Ferdinand Buisson, president of the League of Human Rights to M. Sarraut, minister of the colonies, about the revolt that occurred in 1917 in Thaï N'Guyen (Indochina) and the repression that followed.

In this letter, the role of the Résident of the province, M. Darles is clearly identified: this official, by the abuses of which he was guilty, was principally responsible for the rebellion. His guilt was also established by the Court of Saigon in 1917.

But can you believe it? No administrative sanction has been imposed. On the contrary: M. Darles has been appointed member of the City Council of Saigon. As for judicial sanction, it is a derisory 200 francs fine.

This M. Darles is an administrator of value. He acquired his political science degree in the Latin Quarter where he was a soup merchant.

Per the wishes of an influential politician, M. Darles, then penniless and debt-ridden, was made administrator in Indochina.

Comfortably placed at the head of a Province of several thousand inhabitants and invested with unchecked power: he is Prefect, Mayor, Judge, Bailiff, and tax collector; in a word, he combines all powers. Justice, taxes, property, the lives and goods of natives, the rights of civil servants, elections of mayors and district heads, that is to say the destiny of an entire province is entrusted to the hands of this former mess steward.

Since he could not become rich by extorting his customers in Paris, he takes his revenge in Tonkin by stopping, imprisoning, and arbitrarily convicting the Annamites to squeeze money from them.

Here are some facts that illustrate the despotic reign of this charming administrator that the mother Republic has kindly sent to civilize us.

The indigenous volunteers! are brought into service as riflemen and pass, to that end, a physical. They are the illiterate and intimidated people who Mister Résident berates, punches or strikes with canes if they do not hop to fast enough.

He roughly punched three militiamen who had let a prisoner escape, dragged them on the ground by the hair, banging their heads against the wall of his residence.

For interrogating prisoners, Mister Résident pricked their thighs with his ceremonial sword. Some vanished on their return to prison.

Unfortunate malnourished prisoners, dressed in wretched rags, raised at daybreak, yoked, fastened to one another with large foot shackles, draw the roller, a huge compressor that needed to move on thick layers of sandstone. Completely exhausted, they plod under a relentless sun. The Résident arrives, carrying a usual strong cane, and without reason, by an inconceivably bestial sadism, he strikes with a vengeance those unhappy ones with his stick, accusing them of being lazy.

One day, our civilizer, coming to reproach a European agent and, not knowing on whom to vent his anger, took from his desk an iron ruler and broke two fingers of an unfortunate native writer who had nothing to do with the case.

Another day, he whipped smack in the face, a native sergeant in the presence of his men.

Another time, he buried up to the neck militiamen who displeased him and did not have them dug out until they were half dead.

When he went to the road where he forced the natives to work for one or two pennies a day, after collecting 15 cents from others to exempt them from their day of required labor, there are broken legs by the half-dozens from blows of shovels and pickaxe handles.

One time, in a shipyard, he seized the rifle from a guard to hit a prisoner. The latter having managed to dodge, the Résident turned against the guard who he struck with the same gun. His worthy half, Madame Résident, intervened in her turn; she gladly beat prisoners and was given the opportunity to punish militiamen.

We saw Mister Résident burst the eye of a sergeant with a cane. He has done other great deeds, but we can not list them all here.

All this is known and seen by everyone, including his superiors, Governors-General, and higher Résidents who, to reward his "energy" and his "republican virtue" inflict on him merciless promotions.

III. Messieurs Boudineau, Beaudoin and Others

Despite flashy exhibitions, pompous speeches, royal tours and grandiloquent articles, nothing is going to change in Indochina.

The magistrates dock where the honest administrator Lanon sits is barely cooled when we are told of other scandals on the horizon.

First is the case of Boudineau. Mr. Boudineau is a typical civilizer, a grafting administrator. Among the charges against him, we report this one:

"The village of Tânan, county seat of the Canton, built an electric plant using municipal resources and loans. The operation was successful since the village had revenue largely exceeding the expenditure. Its buildings and streets were also illuminated for free.

"He (Boudineau) is found to be an administrator ingenious enough to force a merger where Tânan village granted its company to a contractor for free so that it could have the pleasure of paying to light its buildings. We see today that there is interest in buying back this franchise given away for free, and the town will have to pay several tens of thousands of piasters. This whole thing is truly a novel in which the former province chief's gifts of imagination were given free reign with unbelievable cynicism."

The second scandal in sight is the case of Théard. Here is what is said Indochina provides:

"We live in really unusual times: the Boudineau deal, the Leno deal and soon the Théard case.

"Mr. Théard, an engineer of great merit, director of a large French firm in Haiphong, to came in to offer an improper advance of ten thousand dollars to Mr. Scala, director of Customs and Excise, to conclude a deal with the administration for opium. He must be guided by such special considerations to think that such a step is not abnormal. This is, in the

Indochinese business world, the common squeeze. All those who have authority will speculate for the greater good of their purse and the greatest harm to the community.

Since Mr. Darles, Résident torturer of Thaï N'Guyen is appointed member of the Saigon municipal council, and Mr. Baudoin, impatiently awaited by Mr. Judge Waren, is made temporary Governor-General of Indochina, the least we can do for Misters Théard and Boudineau is to decorate them.

Chapter V

The Civilizers

A question: Is it true that in the Security Services of the central government of Indochina, there is employed a Frenchman named C…? That C…, on a "mission" to Phy-Xuyen, requires local Annamese to call him Quanlon, "high mandarin", and violently strikes those who do not do so fast enough? Is it true that the same C… raped an Annamite militiaman? Anything goes, anything is possible in this Indochinese paradise.

.
. .

In mid-December 1922, a European deputy sergeant of the Saigon city police – while completely "plastered" – entered a native house and seriously wounded two of its inhabitants, including a woman.

Questioned by the judge, the policeman stated *that he did not remember anything,* but denied that he had been in a state of intoxication.

Witnesses, including a European, argued the contrary, that this *guardian of order* was not in his normal state at the time of the tragic incident.

Whether this civilizer was crazy or drunk or whatever, we wish wholeheartedly that he is decorated for the courageous act he has performed.

•
• •

In the colonies, when one has white skin, he is of the aristocracy: he belongs to a superior race. To maintain his position, the least of European customs agents has at least one domestic, a "boy", who often serves as a "maid of all work."[28]

As the native servant is very malleable and inexpensive, it is not uncommon to find that colonial officials, going home to France on leave or in retirement, bring their domestics with them.

Such is the case of Mr. Jean Le M..arigny, a resident of Carnot Street in Cherbourg. This gentleman, returning from Indochina, brought with him a boy at a salary of 35 francs a month. There is no need to tell you that the native was obliged to toil from morning to night, in addition to being poorly housed and very malnourished. Weekly rest and feast days were unknown in this house.

One day, Mr. Jean Le M..arigny tried to send his "protégé" to dig in the countryside. The son of Annam, who has previously tasted the happy country life that his good boss reserved for him, declined the offer.

So the enraged former civilizer threw the Annamite out the door after having seriously beaten him. Despite repeated claims of the native, Mr. Le M..arigny did not want to give him what belonged to him: money, trunk, clothes, etc… Suddenly thrown on the pavement, ignorant of the language of the country, without resources, without friends, disoriented, this unfortunate person is in terrible misery.

•
• •

The colonial bureaucracy[29] is the principal cause of the expensive life in the colonies. To better understand to what extent this parasitic factor weighs heavily on the budget, and so on the backs of working people:

English India has 4,898 European officials for 325 million people.

French Indochina has 4,300 European officials for 15 million people.

That is to say that there is in the English colony one European official to 66,150 locals and in the French colony there is one European official to 3,490 locals.

In India, the Customs and Excise Administration has 240 European civil servants.

In Indochina, the same administration possesses 1,100 European staff members.

There are in India 26,000 post and telegraph offices with 268 European officials.

Indochina has 330 offices and 340 European employees.

Why the disproportionate amount of budgetivores in Indochina? Because the colony is an earthly paradise where, with a few rare exceptions, all the garbage of politics, of finance, of journalism, etc… spewed out by the metropolis, find a very favorable field for their development… Let's start with the biggest cheese, the Governor-General. Regarding him, an impartial colonist wrote this: "Arriving in Tonkin, Governors have only one goal; to cram the world with friends, sons, parents, political supporters, all those who have an interest in his advancement; often, he is a man riddled with debt, chased by creditors he must repay.

For the noble writer who will write the glorious history of civilizing colonization, the war for so-called law and justice is a source of inexhaustible documentation. Albert Sarraut in a heat of eloquence and enthusiasm says, "Most of the great military leaders who led us to victory were educated in combat in the conquest of the colonial empire, and whose glory and achievements French opinion already celebrated when they carried our flag under African and Asian skies."

As candid in thought, but in less subtle in word choice, *The Journal of Geneva* says straight out "is the difficulty in Geneva?"[30] – Says flatly "the Republic has seen in the establishment of its colonial empire, *a distraction from the defeat of 1870*. The

French race finds in it *revenge for its European woes*, and the military, *a new opportunity* to report in happy combat.

And *go to the devil* if *these testimonials allow you to persist in not believing that colonization* is nothing more or less that a *civilizing and humanitarian mission.*

. . .

1st Five thousand francs was stolen from Mr. Guinaudeau. To obtain confessions from his indigenous employees, this good boss and great civilizer, submitted the latter to electric shocks. It was discovered later that the thief was not a native, but another civilizer: it was the son of Mr. Guinaudeau! Mr. Guineaudeau was acquitted. And the eight unfortunate natives are still in the hospital.

2nd Mr. Vollard, civilizer and trader, did not pay his native employees regularly. One of them asked the foreman for the wages owed. Mr. Vollard gave the foreman the following note: Tell this pig to eat shit, it is the only food for which he is fit."

This happened in Tunisia, in 1923, at the same time that Mr. Millerand made his presidential tour in this country.

. . .

When you have white skin, you are automatically a civilizer. And when one is a civilizer, one can commit savage acts while remaining most civilized.

Thus, a Director of Public Works in Cochinchina forced the Annamese encountered in the street to give him the formal hello due to the superior race by the vanquished race.

One day, a native scribe left work, reading a novel. Coming to a comic passage, the reader began to laugh. Just at this moment, he crossed paths with Mr. Public Works Director who became enraged, first because the native, absorbed in his reading, had not noticed and greeted him; then because the native had allowed himself to laugh while passing a white person. So our civilizer therefore stopped the Annamite and, after requesting his name, asked him if he wanted a slap. Naturally, the scribe declined such a generous offer and expressed the astonishment he felt at such an outburst. Without any form of trial, the official took the native by the coat and dragged him before the chief of the province.

This same Director of Public Works, to align homes and gardens, ordered the people on the edge of provincial roads, under threat of a fine, to remove their trees and clear out their gardens within a time he set.
And one is surprised at the discontent in the colonies!

Not only the Governors and Résidents can do what they like, but customs officials, policemen and all those who have any authority to use and abuse, are certain they can do so with impunity.

A police commissioner in Tuyen-Quang (Tonkin) hit a native and broke his arms.

Another commissioner, this one in Dalat (Cochinchina) has launched a wonderfully interesting trading system that we are happy to bring to the attention of Mr. Dior and Mr. Sarraut. One day, this official needed boards. He sent his militiamen to buy some in town. Buy, is a manner of speaking, as the Commissioner had not given money to his men. They went into town nevertheless, chose wood, and wanted to take it without paying, naturally. The seller would not allow his goods to be taken away without being paid for. The militiamen reported the extraordinary claims of the merchant to their white chief.

Enraged, Mr. Commissioner authorized three armed men to seize the person of this pretentious trader. The latter, being seized, refused to be taken away. The militia returned to notify their superior. Exasperated, Mr. Superintendent doubled the team, ordering them to bring in the stubborn merchant, dead or alive.

The armed guards surrounded the house of the seller and proceeded to execute their orders.

A European businessman intervened on the side of the native merchant and wrote to the Commissioner. But the energetic collaborator of Mr. Long maintained his "summons" and was heard to say that if the native persisted in not coming in, he would be subjected to big trouble.

The native merchant was obliged to leave his business and his country to escape the wrath of the "civilizing" white officer.

⁂

Seven poor Annamese, in a long, thin boat, driven by the current and by the effort of their seven oars each pulled by two arms, was traveling on the water as fast as a steamboat. The sampan of the tax collector, with the French flag flying at the stern, popped out from a stream hidden by mangroves. A sailor shouted to stop; they continued to row. They did not understand. The Customs sampan could hardly go as fast. The customs agent took a Winchester and fired. The bark flew by. Blam! Blam! A rower screamed and fell. Blam! Another. However, a European brickmaker, lurking nearby in a boat, also proceeded to surprise the "pirates" at a bend. Blam! Blam! Blam! He was a good shot. Three bullets, three victims. The boat, with two survivors, was then lost in the streams.

On another day, the same customs agent, followed by six armed sailors, had discovered a poor devil, hidden in a pool, immersed in the mud, breathing through a blowpipe, one end of which was placed in his mouth and the other emerged with leaves of water lilies that had been skillfully arranged on the surface. The customs agent brought the Résident the head of this "pirate", a simple villager who took fright in seeing strangers come toward his village with threatening countenance, armed with revolvers, ammunition pouches, and clutching Winchesters. Found in his boxes were three cartridge casings, Chinese cakes, and a logger's machete. How can we doubt that the man was not a pirate and that the village did not supply the pirates!

A young officer disembarked from France arrived in a village, saw the huts empty and the population gathered in the square. He imagined himself falling into an ambush and fired on this harmless troupe celebrating a religious festival that then dispersed in distress. He followed and exterminated them.

When I arrived in Tonkin, says an old "Tonkinese" do you know what the life of an Annamite was worth on the boats of the great exploiter? Not a sapek![31] That is true.

Look here, I remember when we went up the Red River in our motorboats, we played "absinthe" to see who could "knock down"[32] the most Annamites on the bank in ten rifle shots.

A few, Winchesters in hand, seized villagers and boats for ransom.

A company of marines left for Viahthoung; the mandarin of the country, as a courtesy, came in great pomp with his militia to meet the arrivals. The chief scout of the company ordered his platoon to shoot on the mandarin's escort and harvested several bodies.
When you can not get rid of an insurgent, set fire to his village. Thus was the area around Hunghao razed.

On a hidden trail, there was a yellow man who staggered because he was carrying two big baskets of peanuts, with the help of a stick across the shoulders. He did not run away at our approach. He was taken and shot.

We spend all day tapping with a stick or the flat of a sword on the Annamese, to make them work.

The Annamese are very soft, very submissive; but we talk to them only with kicks in the c...

The Annamite patriots are considered brigands. This is how Doi-Van, patriot who had fought against foreign domination for several years, was beheaded in Hanoi, his head displayed in Bachnin, and his body thrown into the Red River.

Ton-duy-Tan, taken after ten years of desperate struggle, is condemned and beheaded.

Phan-dinh-Phung, a high mandarin, resisted for ten years, he finally died in the forest. His death was not enough; his body was exhumed and the remains scattered; he was pursued beyond the grave.

In the province of Quangtri, an alcoholic overseer of public works "dismounted" from his elephant with a rifle shot, a native who was guilty of not having heard or understood his orders.

An equally alcoholic customs official slaughtered, with blows to the spleen from a club, an Annamite sailor assigned to duty in Baria (Cochinchina).

A French contractor killed a militiaman in Dalat where, it goes without saying, a native carpenter likewise died, following violence from another civilizer.

A contractor required its workers to work night and day in the water to build a tunnel; many die and the rest go on strike. The contractor, in person, set fire to the strikers' houses to force them back to work. An entire village was burned in the dead of night.

A chief warrant officer of artillery set fire to a house on the pretext that the owner, whose husband was away, would not receive him at midnight. The poor woman was naturally terrified.

A polygamous lieutenant threw a young woman down and knocked her out with blows from a rattan cane because she did not want to live with him.

An officer of the Navy yard murdered an Annamite railway employee, pushing him into a blazing fire after a severe beating.

.
. .

There is not in the world, wrote Vigne d'Octon, conquered people who are subject to more abuse and mistreatment than the native.

Another traveler wrote: "Colonial life just develops defects in the individual: lack of moral sense, debauchery and dishonesty, cruelty toward those who have seen war; among camp followers and other adventurers, a taste for rape and theft. In France, an opportunity to do this was missing, and the fear of the police was stronger! Here, these chaps are sometimes alone with a few natives, on their junk or in some village; they are more like looters than

Europeans at the market and more brutal toward the peasants who protest.

All the French, wrote a third, come here with the idea that the Annamites are their inferiors and must serve as their slaves. They treat them like beasts best to be driven with the stick. All of them have become accustomed to regarding themselves as members of a new and privileged aristocracy. Whether military or settlers, they do not usually conceive of other kinds of relationships with the natives than those they employ with their servants. It seems that the boy[33] is to them the representative of the whole yellow race. It should be understood with what simple scorn the French of Indochina speaks of the "yellow." It should be seen with what rudeness the Europeans treat the natives.

The conqueror attaches great importance to signs of submission or respect from the conquered. The Annamites of the cities, like those in the countryside, are obliged to remove their hats to a European.

A safety officer brutally strikes Annamites who forget to treat him like a Grand Mandarin. A customs clerk requires the natives passing by his house to remove their hats or get down from their mounts. One day, this civilizer brutalized an Annamite woman who had greeted him but had forgotten to address him as a High Mandarin. This woman was pregnant. The violent kick that the agent gave her right in the stomach caused an abortion; the unfortunate died shortly after that.

If our protectors insist that Annamese be humble, submissive, docile and polite, all the same, "it seems to take nothing to make our presence obnoxiously unbearable" said a writer who visited Indochina. And he continues: "In Europe, the yellow race is regarded as having all guile and all deceit. Yet, we care very little to esteem our own rights."

These officers pull the beard of the bonzes during services. One son of an influential father beat an Annamite official because, though he was the first occupant, did not want to give up his seat on the bus.

Upon arrival of the Governor-General in Marseilles, at a lunch in his honor, it was proposed to bring the Annamite Mandarins to stay in this city. "If the Mandarins are brought, replied the Commissioner-General of Indochina, I will bring my boy."

．
． ．

We quote the following fact from the travel journal of a colonial soldier:

While the "Tonkinese" entertain themselves, on the starboard side some junks sell fruits and shellfish. To get to us, the Annamese lift long poles fitted with baskets that had their goods. We need bother only to choose. As money, those who allow themselves the luxury of paying, deposit at the bottom of these baskets the most diverse objects: pipe cleaners, buttons, and cigarette butts. (This is, perhaps, how commercial honesty is taught to the natives!) Sometimes, here's a funny story, some drivers throw a bucket of boiling water on the backs of the poor. Then there are screams of pain, and a wild panic of rowing making canoes collide.

Just below me an Annamite, BURNED FROM HEAD TO FOOT, absolutely crazy, wants to jump into the sea. His brother, forgetting the danger, drops the oar, grabs him, and forces him to the bottom of the sampan. The fight, which did not last two seconds, is hardly over when another bucket of water, launched with a steady hand, SCALDED THE SAVIOR IN TURN. I saw him rolling in his boat with inhuman cries, his flesh raw! And that makes us laugh, it seems exceedingly funny. WE HAVE ALREADY THE COLONIAL SOUL!

And further:

When I was there (Tonkin) we hardly spent a week without seeing some heads fall.

Of these spectacles, I have retained but one thing, it is that we are crueler, more barbarous than the pirates themselves. Why these delicacies toward the convicted person who is going to die? Why the physical torture, and these prisoner processions through the villages?

⁎
⁎ ⁎

Mr. Doumier, former Governor-General of Indochina, delivered these solemn words at a meeting of the Chamber of Deputies: "I knew the police in the colonies, and I even expanded the number of brigades, having found it was the police force that gave natives the guarantee of protection against the possibility of abusive actions by some settlers. *The policemen were popular among the natives.*

We will see how the policemen meant to fabricate "their popularity." Let us say at once that they are very mild and paternal to criminals, it is a fact. But to the peaceful natives, that's another story. Not to mention, for the time being, the painful case of the Central Prison of Saigon, where, in 1916 [34], pushed by a highly patriotic zeal, the police indiscriminately stopped gentlemen, without rhyme or reason, and the innocents thus arrested were condemned and executed. Even if the Annamite blood that reddens the Plain of Tombs fades with time, the wounded hearts of widows, orphans and mothers will never be healed. The culprits, including the police who were the vile instruments, are not punished, and justice is not yet done. Today, we point out just a few individual cases.

A commissioner of Tonkin, on the pretext of maintaining the cleanliness of the gutters, walks all day along the flow paths and as soon as he sees the smallest blade of grass in the water, hands out innumerable punishments and fines to the unfortunate inhabitants of the place.

To avoid accidents in waterways in the west of Cochinchina, a flotilla of borrowed river craft was used to install a police checkpoint in each channel with the mission of preventing junks slipping by too fast or obstructing traffic. With the presence of the police, a veritable sluice gate of fines and tickets is opened on them. Almost all the junks passing through these waters are having fines imposed on them ranging from one to two piasters. To crushing taxes collected by the state is also a right of toll established by the "popular" policeman, and the Annamite is happy, very happy!

Besides, preferment awaits the most zealous,

as it appears that the gentlemen of the police are entitled to a 20% commission on the yield of the fines! What a beautiful system!

A native newspaper said that "the indigenous population does not want more French policemen who are too often a calamity for honest people."

. . .

A certain Mr. Pourcignon rushed furiously at an Annamite who had the curiosity and audacity to look for a few seconds at the house of the European. He struck and finally felled him with a pistol shot in the head.

. . .

A railroad employee struck a Tonkinese village chief with strokes of a cane, stopped him, and locked him up in a dog cage.

Mr. Beck split his chauffeur's skull with a punch.

Mr. Bres, an entrepreneur, killed with kicks an Annamite whose arms he tied together, after having him bitten by his dog.

Mr. Deffis, tax collector, killed his Annamite domestic with a formidable kick in the kidneys.

Mr. Henry, mechanic, heard noises in the street; the door of his house opened; and an Annamite woman entered, pursued by a native. Henry, who believed that the individual was pursuing his own *daughter*[35], grabbed a shotgun and fired. The individual dropped dead.

A Frenchman tied his horse in a stable where there was the mare of a native. The horse reared, causing a blind rage in the Frenchman. He hit the native until blood flowed from his mouth and ears. After that, he garroted him and hung him in the staircase.

A missionary (ah yes! a gentle apostle) suspecting his native seminarian of stealing 1,000 piasters, tied him up, suspended him from a frame, and struck him. The poor man fainted. He was taken down. When he came to, it started again. The native was dying. He may be dead today.

Etc…, etc.

Has justice punished these individuals, these civilizers?

Some were acquitted, and the others were not even worried.

After seeing three natives graze their sheep in his olive trees, a French settler sent his wife to get a rifle and cartridges. He ambushed them in a thicket, fired three times and severely wounded the three natives.

Another French colonist had in his service two native workers, Amdouni and Ben-Belkhir. They had, it seems, stolen some grapes. The colonist sent for the natives and beat them with a blackjack until they fainted. When they regained consciousness, our protector bound them, arms in back, and hung them by their hands. Although both unfortunates lost consciousness, this heinous torture continued for four hours and ended only when a neighbor protested.

Carried to the hospital, they each had one hand amputated. It is not certain that the other hand can be saved.

•
• •

An Annamite, 50 years of age, and employed for 25 years in the service of the railways of Cochinchina, was murdered by a white officer. Here are the facts: Lé-Van-Taï had four other Annamites under him. Their function was to close the bridge for passing trains and open it to inland watercraft. Regulations required the closure of the bridge ten minutes before the trains pass.

On April 2nd, 4:30 p.m., an Annamese had closed the bridge and lowered the signal. Just then an *administrative officer of the Navy Yard came by, returning from hunting.* The boat began to whistle.

55

The native employee ran to the middle of the bridge, waving his red flag to make it clear to the officers of the little steamboat that the train was about to pass. But then the boat came alongside a bridge pier. The officer jumped out and walked angrily toward the Annamite. The latter prudently ran off toward the house of his manager, Taï. The officer pursued, throwing stones. After hearing the noise, Taï left his house and went to meet the representative of civilization who yelled at him, "Idiot! Why didn't you open it?" In response, Taï, who can not speak French, pointed to the red flag. This simple gesture infuriated the associate of Mr. Long who, without further ado, fell on Taï and *after having given him a good "thrashing"*,[36] pushed him into a brazier fire that was nearby.

Horribly burned, the Annamite gatekeeper was taken to the hospital, where he died after six days of agony.

The official was not worried. In Marseilles, the prosperity of Indochina is officially exhibited, but in Annam, we are starving. In France, we sing of loyalty, there, we are murdered!
While the life of an Annamite dog is not worth a sapeck[31], for a scratch on the arm Mr. inspector general Reinhart receives 120,000 francs compensation.

.
. .

The civilizing of Moroccans by cannon fire continues.

A commander of Zouaves,[37] garrisoned at Settat, addressing the soldiers, said: "We must finish with these savages. Morocco is rich in agricultural and mineral products. We, civilized French, are here for two purposes: to civilize *and to enrich ourselves*."

This commander was right. He, above all, has the candor to admit that, if you go to the colonies, it is to steal from the natives. Because, after only ten years of the protectorate, 379,000 hectares of arable land in Morocco is occupied by Europeans, 368,000 by French civilizers. The area of the colony being 815,000 square kilometers, if civilization continues its march; in a few years, the unfortunate Moroccan will no longer have in his country an inch of land free for him to live on and work without suffering under the yoke of exploitative and enslaving colonialism.

CHAPTER VI

Administrative Mismanagement

The budget of Cochinchina, for example, amounted to 5,561,680 piasters (12,791,000 francs) in 1911; it was 7,321,817 piasters (16,840,000 francs) in 1912. In 1922, it amounted to 12,821,325 piasters (96,169,000 francs). A simple calculation shows that between 1911 and 1922 there was a difference of 83,369,000 francs in the budget of this colony. Where does the money go? Simply to staff costs that devour almost 100% of total revenue.

Other splurges are added one to another to waste money that has been sweated out of poor Annamites. It is not yet known the exact number of piasters spent on the ride of the King of Annam to France, but we know that, in awaiting the auspicious day, the only one when the Emperor[38] could embark, the liner *Porthos* had to be compensated for four days of delay at 100,000 francs per day (400,000 francs). Travel, 400,000 francs. The reception cost 240,000 (besides the salaries of police officers to monitor the Annamese in France). To lodge the Annamite militiamen in Marseilles to "present arms" to His Excellency and His Majesty, 77,600 francs.

Since we are in Marseilles, let's take advantage of it to see what the colonial exposition cost. Firstly, and apart from those who are supported in the metropole,[39] thirty officials were brought from the colonies who, while they sip aperitifs at the Cannebière Hotel, draw salaries both at the exhibition and in the colonies. Indochina alone had to spend 12 million for this exhibition. And do you know how this money was spent? Here is an example: the famous reconstruction of the palaces of Angkor required 3,000 cubic meters of timber at 400 or 500 francs per meter. Total 1.2 to 1.5 million francs!

Other examples of waste. Automobiles and luxury cars were not enough for carrying Mister Governor-General, he needed a special railcar: modifications to this car cost the Treasury 125,250 francs.

In eleven months of the year, the Economic Agency (?) has charged the economies of Indochina a sum of 464,000 francs.

At the colonial school, where future civilizers are made, forty-four professors of all categories are funded for 30 or 35 students. Even more thousands of francs.

The annual budgetary cost of defense works inspections in the colony is 785,168 francs. Now, the gentlemen inspectors never left Paris and knew no more about the colonies than they knew about the old moon.

In other colonies, we find the same mismanagement. To receive an unofficial "economic" mission, the treasury of Martinique is "relieved" of 40,000 francs. In the space of 10 years, the budget of Morocco went from 17 to 290 million francs, although it reduced by 30% expenditure of local interest, that is to say, the expenses that would have benefited the natives!

•
• •

Returning from a visit to the colonies, a former deputy cried out, "The highway robbers are honest people compared to the officials of our colonies!" Although favored by huge salaries, (a European agent, even illiterate, starts at 200 piasters = 2,000 francs) these gentlemen are never satisfied. They want to earn more, by every means.

Scholarships were awarded to the sons of fathers, résidents or administrators in service, who profited from their positions and receive low wages (40,000 to 100,000 francs).

Some sessions of the Colonial Council were virtually devoted solely to the systematic looting of the budget. One chairman had almost two million francs of subcontracted work on his own. A director of the Internal Affairs, who represented the government in the Council, requested and received double his salary. The making of a road, drawn out from year to year and performed without oversight, was the third source of regular profit. Fourth, the position of medical officers for the colonies received serious emoluments. The fifth is doctor of municipal services; the sixth is the supplier of stationery and official printer. And so on.

If the coffer sounds somewhat empty, it certainly did not take long to refill it. On their own authority, they warned the natives that they needed a certain amount. The burden was spread among the villages that were eager to perform so as not to incur immediate reprisals.

When a Résident-General had any expense to settle, he issued mandarin's certificates. One told of a province where an operation of this kind was done to the tune of 10,620 francs. And these facts were not rare at all.

One of our senior Résidents, whose credits for a boat were spent a few months too early, was reimbursed for the expenses of I know not what celebration, where the King would be invited to the launch.

The traveling salesmen of civilization and democracy are familiar with the D system.[40]

∴

A former Governor-General of Indochina admitted one day that this colony was covered with too many unnecessary staff for its budget.

A good half of these officials, province chiefs or others, satisfy in only a very imperfect manner the qualifications of men who are conferred with such broad and formidable powers, wrote a colonial.

They all were good at wasting public money, and the poor Annamite wretches paid, always paid. They paid not only officials whose functions were useless, but they also paid employees whose jobs did not exist! In 19..., 250,000 francs thus evaporated.

For the movement of His Excellency, a warship was assigned. The fittings amounted to 250,000 francs, not counting the "incidental expenses" which cost Indochina over 80,000 francs for each trip.

The Governor was not satisfied with the sumptuous palaces he inhabited in Saigon and Hanoi: he needed a villa by the sea. Again, it was Indochina who "shelled out."

In 19... when some John Doe or other type of foreigner went to Saigon, the Governor received him in a princely manner. For four days, it was a riot of parties, gluttony, and champagne; poor Cochinchina paid the bill: 75,000 francs.

Administrators were small potentates, who like to surround themselves with luxury and sumptuousness to enhance, they said, their prestige vis-à-vis the native. A Résident created a company of lancers to be his guard and never went without an escort. In all the Residences, one found 6 to 11 horses, 5 or 6 carriages: victorias, tilburys, mylords, malabars, etc. To these already superfluous means of transport, luxurious automobiles costing tens of thousands of piasters were added in the budget. Some administrators even maintained a racing stable.

These gentlemen were housed, furnished, and illuminated at the cost of a princess; on top of that, their coachmen, their drivers, their stable hands, their gardeners, in a word their servants were paid by the administration.

Literary distractions themselves were provided free of charge to those happy people. One such director budgeted 900 piasters for his heating![41] And 1,700 piasters of costs for newspaper subscriptions! Another managed to transform a set of accounts: the purchase of dresses, pianos, and toilet articles, into the buying of materials for the upkeep of the Residence or similar classifications, to be paid by the state budget!

.
. .

Whether they were soup merchants or imperious intellectual pedants in school, once they arrived in the colonies, our civilizers led lives of princes. One administrator used five or six militiamen to keep goats. Another had militiamen sculptors making pretty figurines of Buddha or elegant trunks of camphor wood.

We mentioned the case of a brigade inspector for whom the regulations allowed only

one militiaman as an orderly, and he employed:

one Sergeant factotum, one steward, three boys, two cooks, three gardeners, one valet, one coachman, and a groom.

And Madame had in her service: one tailor, two launderers, one embroiderer, one weaver.

The child had a special boy who never left him.

A witness cited a meal at a director's – an ordinary meal and not a banquet – where each guest had a militiaman behind him to change his plates and pass him the courses. And all the militia in the room were placed under the command of a sergeant-major.

CHAPTER VII

The Exploitation of Natives

After stealing fertile land, the French sharks collected taxes on bad land a hundred times more outrageous than the feudal taxes –

Vigne d'Octon

Before our occupation, the property tax roll for all the communal and individual lands within the villages was by crop category. The tax rate ranged from 1 piaster to 50 cents for rice paddies. For the other fields, 1.40 piasters to 12 cents. The unit area was the square Mau, 150 Thuoc per side. The length of the Thuoc varied. It was, by province, 42, 47 and 64 centimeters and the corresponding areas of the Mau were 3,970; 4,900 and 6,200 square meters.

To increase State revenues, a length of 40 centimeters was taken as the basis of all measurements, less than all the units of measure used. The area of a Mau was thus fixed at 3,600 square meters. Property taxes were increased by that amount in proportion, and varied by province: a twelfth in some localities, a third in others, two-thirds in the less favored.

From 1890 to 1896, direct taxes doubled; from 1896 to 1898, they increased again by half. When an increase was imposed on a village, it resigned itself and paid: to whom could it have brought its complaints? The success of these operations encouraged Résidents to repeat them. In the eyes of many Frenchmen, the docility of the town was clear proof that the measure was not excessive!

.
. .

The head tax went from 14 cents to 2 piasters and 50 cents. The unregistered, that is to say, the young people under 18, who had to pay nothing before, were subject to a tax of 30 cents, or more than twice that paid previously by the registered.

According to a decree of the Résident-Superior of Tonkin dated December 11, 1919, all natives aged 18 to 60 years old were subject to a unique personal tax of 2 piasters and 50 cents.

Each Annamite is required always to carry an identity card and present it on request. Whoever forgets or misplaces this card is arrested and imprisoned.

To address the decline in piasters, the Governor-General Doumer had simply increased the number of registered taxable!

Every year each village was assigned a number of registered and a certain extent of land of various categories when additional resources were wanted. Figures changed during the year; villages were forced to pay on a greater enrollment and larger land area than had been given out at the beginning of the year. Thus in the province of Nam-Dinh (Tonkin) whose total area did not reach 120,000 hectares, the figures mentioned 122,000 hectares of rice paddies and the Annamite was forced to pay the tax on land that did not exist! If he cried, no one heard.

Taxes were not only overwhelming, but they varied each day.

It was the same with certain rights of movement. It was impossible, however, to equitably collect taxes of this kind. A permit is issued for 150 kilos of tobacco, and this same product is taxed several times in succession; when it changes ownership, and when the 150 kilos are divided between three or four different buyers. The only rules are the imagination of the customs agents. They inspire such fear that the Annamites, on seeing them, abandon on the road the basket of salt, tobacco or betel that he was carrying. He would rather give up his goods than pay eternal fees. In some regions, it was necessary to tear out the tobacco plants and throw the areca palms on the ground, to not put up with the trouble caused from a new tax.

In Luang-Prabang (Laos), lamentable paupers loaded with irons were used for cleaning roads. They were guilty only of being unable to pay.

After being devastated by flooding, the province of Bac-Ninh (Tonkin) was still forced to pay 500,000 piasters in taxes.

•
• •

You have heard Mr. Maurice Long, Governor-General of Indochina, Mr. Albert Sarraut, Colonial Secretary and their press – a disinterested press – trumpeting the success of the Indochinese loan. However, they did not to tell you by what means they have achieved this success. They may have been right not to disclose their professional secret, and that secret was this: First, the dupes are lured with the promise of profits. As it did not yield enough, the villages were robbed of their communal property. It was still not enough; so the wealthy natives were brought in, given a receipt in advance, and they had only to extricate themselves by paying the listed amounts. As the government till is deep and industrial and native traders not many, these compulsory loans did not fill those unfathomable depths. Then the borrower State, tapped on the heap of those most tapped out: it required two, three, four or more fellows to subscribe to a common share!

Here, for example, was a trick that administrators employed to subtract money from the pockets of the togged[42] natives.

It was in a province of the West, a few weeks before the offering of the Indochinese loan.

The chief of this province met the canton chiefs under his jurisdiction, and after explaining the terms of the loan through an interpreter, said to them in conclusion:

- "Here, my duty is to give you the explanation.

Subscribe now!

While informing a canton chief standing next to him, the distinguished "quan-lon"[43] asked:

- And you, what can you raise from your Canton?

The poor man, caught off-guard by the question, stammered a few words to make it understood that he could not give figures, having not yet seen his citizens to determine their potential contributions.

- Close your m…. You are not worthy of your duties. You're fired!

………………………………………………………

The loan is floated. The Governor of Cochinchina, during his tour, stops at the province capital and asked about the amount raised for the week.

- 73,000 piasters! They told him.

The governor did not seem happy with the figure, as the province is deemed the richest in western Cochinchina, and it did more than that in the last loan.

After the departure of the head of the colony, the province chief decides to make a promotional tour of his fief. He sees all the rich natives with a firearm. To each he sets an amount, and, to make it clear to the complainant that it is not for fun, he confiscates his gun.

- You know, if you do not pay up, we will not return your weapon!

And the people perform.

Incidentally, the same administrator spent 30,000 piasters to build a 9-kilometer road that is collapsing into a nearby canal. We hope the Trans-Indochina railroad[44] has a better fate.

∴

A pagoda was under construction. The workforce was provided by prisoners under the direction of a notable. On the daily worksheet, the day laborers were regularly paid by contractors. But it was Mr. Résident who pocketed the money.

Mr. Résident had been decorated. To celebrate his decoration, a public subscription was started. The specific amounts of the donations were set for officials, agents, and notables, the minimum was six piasters. Sum collected: 10,000 piasters. A beautiful rosette,[45] is it not?

Providing for construction of wooden bridges and communal schools had left to our honest administrator a small tip of about 2, 000 piasters.

Registration of the animals being free, Mr. Résident permits his employees to collect from .5 to 5 piasters per registered head. In exchange, he receives from them a monthly pension of 200 piasters.

A faked classification of rice paddies also returns to the official – now decorated – 4,000 piasters.

An illegal concession of some hectares of land adds 2,000 piasters to the Résidential till.

Civilizer, super-patriot, Mr. Résident widely took advantage of Victory loans: some villages subscribed to the loan of 1920 – note that we have a loan for each win and a win for each year – for 55,900 francs, at 10 fr. 25 per piaster, makes 5,466 piasters. In 1921, the piaster had fallen to 6 francs, Mr. Résident generously took all such securities from their accounts and paid them 5,466 piasters. He banked 9,325 piasters later, following a further increase [in the value of the piaster].[46]

⁘

We note in the *Official Journal*, 1st session of December 22, 1922, the following fact:

"During the war, the African infantrymen had sent home money orders which, often, made up considerable sums. *These money orders never reached the intended recipients.*

A colleague has just recently reported a similar "phenomenon." This time, it is about Réunion. For months, the Islanders were not able to receive any packages destined for them.

"Such a phenomenon, the newspaper said, surprised both those sending and those who were not receiving.

"There have been complaints. There was an investigation and this, hardly begun, leads to the explanation of the mystery, the discovery of a series of robberies committed with a rather remarkable industriousness and consistency.

"We arrested an employee, then another, then a manager, finally, when all the employees were behind bars, the director joined his staff in prison.

"Every day, the investigation revealed something new. There were more than 125,000 francs worth of stolen packages, the accounting was faked and such a mess that restoring order in the accounts would have required more than six months.

"If we can sometimes find a dishonest employee in an administration, it is rare that an entire department, from the top to the bottom of the ladder, catches the contagion; but what is stranger, *is all this gang of thieves has been operating for several years without being disturbed.*"

.

•
• •

On the occasion of the discussion of the draft law on military aircraft, expenses for which the colonies, that is to say the natives, will be forced to cough up (Indochina 375,000 francs, West Africa 100,000 francs), Mr. Morinaud, deputy from Algeria, said:

"On this occasion, allow me, ladies and gentlemen, after all the congratulations that were sent to them, including the *Times*, who called it a miraculous fact, it is our turn to provide a tribute of admiration for the brave French who have just completed such a great achievement, a tribute that deserves to be shared by *Mr. Citroën, selfless industrialist*, who was quick to supply them with financial and technical resources. (*Applause.*)

"What happened the day after the great event? *It is that the military posts that we have in southern Algeria immediately ordered these unparalleled means of transport for the Sahara, known as caterpillar cars.*

"*The posts of Touggourt and of Ouargla* - this information was provided to me in recent days by the Governor of Algeria – *just ordered two.*

"*All our other forts will, of course, be quickly provided with them.*

"It is necessary, in the short term, to set up some four or five more, so that they are within 200 kilometers of one another.

"New posts will therefore be created. They soon will order caterpillar cars. Thus, all Saharan forts will communicate easily with each other. They will ensure their supplies from post to post with amazing ease. They regularly will receive their mail. (*Applause.*)

(From the *Official Journal*, Jan. 22, 1923.)

•
• •

Corvée[47] workers are not only used to neaten up walkways around homes for the contentment of the Europeans; these forced laborers, who are always at the mercy of the Résidents, also perform more strenuous work.

At the mere announcement of the Minister of Colonies' trip to Indochina, 10,000 men were raised to complete the railway line of V. L., he was to inaugurate.

During the summer of 18.., some time before the famine which desolated the center of Annam, 10,000 Annamites, led by the mayors of their towns, were requisitioned to dredge a channel. A good portion of this enormous labor force found itself without work; it was still kept away from the rice paddies for months at the time when the presence of so many idle hands were indispensable in the fields. It should be noted that such an army had never been gathered when it concerned warding off a public calamity; at the end of 18…, most of the unfortunates who perished from hunger in Annam would have been saved, if someone had organized a transport service from Tourane to provision the areas where the famine was rampant; the 10,000 Annamites at the canal would have been able, in a month, to distribute 2,000 tons of rice in their provinces.

The work on the Tourane road and those of Tran-Ninh and of Ai-Lao left painful memories. The forced laborers had to travel one hundred kilometers before reaching the sites. Then they were housed in appalling huts. Zero hygiene; disorganized medical services; no relief or no shelter on the road. They received insufficient rations of rice, a little dried fish, unhealthy drinking water and they dreaded the mountains. Diseases, fatigue, and ill-treatment caused great mortality.

If the forced laborers were replaced by requisitions, there was but one difference between the two systems, it was that the duration of forced labor was limited and that of requisitions was not. Both met all needs: if customs wanted to move salt, it commandeered boats; if it built a warehouse, workers and materials were requisitioned at the same time.

Requisition was a particularly ill-disguised deportation. Without taking into account farming and religious festivals, it drained off whole communities to work sites. Only a small number returned and, for that matter, nothing was done to ensure their return.

On their way to Lanabion, on their way to the mountains where death awaited them, fed sparingly, even going days without food, laborers forced or requisitioned, deserted or rebelled by the whole convoy, causing terrible repression from the guards and dotting the road with their dead bodies.

The administration of Quangchou-Wan received instructions from the government to recruit. For this occasion, it captured all the natives who worked on the piers. They were tied up and thrown into the conveying vessel.

The inhabitants of Laos, indigenous poor, lived in constant fear of forced labor. When the recruitment officers arrived in front of the huts, they found the huts empty.

At Thydau-Mot, an administrator determined that he needs a steamroller. What did he do? He made an arrangement with a concession company that sought cheap labor. The company bought the roller and delivered it to the administrator for the price of 13,500 francs. The administrator required an impressment of his constituents for the benefit of the company, agreeing that the day of a forced laborer was worth 50 cents. For three years, the inhabitants of Thydau were made available to work for the company. They paid in forced labor for the roller that it pleased Mr. Administrator to buy for his garden.

In another place, the forced laborers, their day finished, were required for free to transport over a distance of one kilometer the stones for building the wall surrounding the administrator's hotel.

At any time, the Annamite could thus be taken away, forced to do the worst chores, malnourished, poorly paid, requisitioned for an unlimited time, and abandoned hundreds of kilometers from his village.

∴

The Annamites, in general, were crushed by the benefits of French protection. The Annamite peasants, in particular, were even more shamefully ground down by this protection: they were oppressed as Annamese; as peasants, they were expropriated. They were the ones who were the forced laborers, who produced for the whole band of parasites, the civilizers and others. They were living in poverty when there was abundance for their executioners; and starved when there was crop failure. They were robbed on all sides, in every way, by the administration, by modern feudalism, by the Church. Formerly, under the Annamese system, the land was divided into several categories, according to its productive capacity. The tax was based on this classification. Under the colonial regime, this was changed. When the French government wanted to find the money, it simply changed the categories. With the stroke of a magic pen, it transformed a barren land into fertile land.

That was not all. It artificially increased the amount of land by reducing the unit of measurement. For this reason, the tax was automatically increased by a third in some places, two-thirds in others. This was not enough to appease the greed of the protector State that raised taxes every year. Thus, from 1890 to 1896, taxes doubled. They had increased by half from 1896 to 1898, and so on. The Annamites were always allowed to be fleeced, and, encouraged by the success of these operations, our protectors continued their grift.

In 1895, the administrator of a province in Tonkin robbed a village of several hectares for the benefit of another village, a Catholic one. The dispossessed complained. They were put in prison. Do not think that the administrative cynicism stopped there. The unfortunates who had been robbed were still obliged to pay until 1910 taxes on the land they had lost in 1895!

After the thieving government, concessionaires were the robbers. The government gave Europeans who had only a big belly and white skin concessions we had heard exceeded 20,000 hectares.

These concessions were based mostly on legalized thefts. During the conquest, the Annamite peasants – like the Alsacians in 1870 – had abandoned their lands to take refuge in the part of the country that was free. When they returned their lands were "concessioned". Entire villages were dispossessed and the natives were reduced to working for the lords of a modern feudalism which sometimes appropriates up to 90% of the harvest.

Under the pretext of encouraging colonization, a large number of the big grant holders were exempt from property tax.

After obtaining free land, the concessionaires got a free, or almost free workforce. The administration supplied them with a number of convicts who worked for nothing, or at the least, it used its influence to recruit workers who were given starvation wages. If the workers did not become numerous enough, or if they were not happy, violence was resorted to; the grant holders seized the mayors and the notables of the villages, bastinadoed and tortured them until they had signed a contract committing them to provide the number of workers required.

In addition to this temporal power, there were spiritual saviors who, while preaching to the Annamites the virtue of poverty, nonetheless sought to enrich themselves by the sweat and the blood of the natives. In Cochinchina, the Saint Apostolic Mission alone had 1/5th of the rice paddies of the country. Although it was not taught by the Bible, the way these lands were acquired was very simple: it was usury and corruption. The Mission benefited from crop failures by lending money to farmers and requiring them to put up their land as collateral. The lending rate was usurious; when the Annamese could not pay when due, the pledged lands then belonged permanently to the Mission.

The supposedly superior governors, to whom the motherland entrusted the fate of Indochina, were generally ignorant or villains. It was enough for the Mission to possess a few private papers, personal, and compromising, to scare the sparrows and get from them everything it wanted. Thus, a Governor-General granted to the Mission 7,000 hectares of waterfront land belonging to indigenous people who, with one stroke, were condemned to begging.

With this brief overview, we see that, under the mask of democracy, French imperialism transplanted the accursed system of the Middle Ages to the country of Annam, where the Annamite peasant is crucified by the bayonet of capitalist civilization and by the cross of prostituted Christianity.

•
• •

Algeria was suffering from famine. Tunisia was ravaged by the same plague. To remedy this situation, the Administration had arrested and imprisoned a large number of the hungry. And so that the "starving" do not take prison for a sanctuary, they were not given anything to eat. They were dying of starvation during imprisonment. In the caves of El Ghiria, the hungry nibbled the carrion of a dead donkey for several days.

In Beja, sharecroppers[48] fight with crows for dead animals.

In El Arba market, in Ghida, in Oued Mlize, the natives died of starvation every day, by the dozens.

With starvation, typhus broke out in several areas and threatened to spread.

⁂

To hide the ugliness of its regime of criminal exploitation, colonial capitalism still decorates its rotten coat of arms with the idealistic motto: Fraternity, equality, etc.

In the same workshop and for the same work, the white worker was paid several times better than his brother of color.

In government, the indigenous, despite their length of service and despite proven ability, received starvation wages, while a white who had recently had strings pulled for him received a higher salary with less work.

Uprooted from their land, their homes, and regimented by force as "volunteers", the militarized natives were quick to savor exquisite "equality".

At the same rank of the native, the white is almost always considered a superior. This "ethno-military" hierarchy is even more striking when the white soldiers and colored soldiers travel together on a train or boat.

⁂

Young natives, who studied in the schools of metropolitan France and obtained their doctorate in medicine or law, could not practice their profession in their own country if they were not naturalized and

God only knows what difficulties the native would encounter, what humiliating steps he must fulfill, before obtaining naturalization.

How could a native become naturalized?

The Act of March 25, 1915, relating to the acquisition of French citizenship by French subjects, tells us this:

Art. 1st – The following may be, after the age of 21 years, enjoy the rights of a French citizen: a subject of or French-protected from Algeria, Tunisia or Morocco, who has established his residence in France, in Algeria or in a country under the protectorate of the Republic, and who meets the following conditions:

1st Has obtained the cross of the Legion of Honor or one of the diplomas of university or professional studies; the list will be decided by decree.

2nd Has rendered important services to colonization or to the interests of France.

3rd Has served in the French army and has acquired either the rank of officer, NCO, or the military medal.

4th Has married a French woman and has one year of residence.

5th Has lived more than ten years in the said countries and has sufficient knowledge of the French language.

In spite of the insufficiency of this law, it passes muster if honestly applied; but no, as prying fools, distinguished officials sit down and require applicants for naturalization to respond in writing to the following questions:

A – Your wife and children, do they speak French?

B – Do they dress like a European?

C – Do you have furniture in your home?

D – And chairs?

E – Do you eat at the table or on the mat?

F – What do you eat?

G – Do you eat rice or bread?

H – Do you own property?

I – And your wife?

J – What is the income from your profession?

K – Your religion?

L – To which groups do you belong?

N – What are your duties in these societies?

O – Why are you asking for naturalization, indigenous status being good and sweet. Is it to be an official? To be important? Or to prospect for gold and ore?

P – Who are your closest friends?

A little more, and these gentlemen will ask us if our wife made l… to us?

•
• •

CHAPTER VIII

Justice

Is it true that, from excess of humanitarian feeling, so often proclaimed by Mr. Sarraut, we did, in the prison of Nha-Trang (Annam), put the inmates on a dry diet, that is to say they were deprived of water for meals? Is it true that we smeared the noses of prisoners with tincture of iodine to make them more easily identifiable in case of escape?

•
• •

About the precautions that were taken to combat the "plague," the July 13, 1921, *Independent* of Madagascar, published a report whose excerpts follow:

A number of huts were burned last Monday, including a quite beautiful one, that of Rakotomanga on Gallieni Street. The hut of Mr. Desraux did not have the same fate, its estimated worth was too high, 50,000 francs with all its contents; accordingly, it was decided that it would be simply disinfected, and it would be forbidden to live in it for a long time, six months we believe."

We add that Mr. Desraux is a French citizen while Rakotomanga is a subject because he is a native. We remind our readers that the law of 1841[49] had been passed for all French farmers.

．
． ．

In Madagascar, six natives were arrested on the concession of a colonist for not having paid their taxes. In court, the defendants state that the settler who employed them, Mr. de la Roche, promised: 1st to pay their taxes; 2nd to exempt them from the performance of public services, and 3rd to give them 10 francs in salary for 30 days of work. It should be noted that this colonist employed them for only one day a week. To meet their needs, these natives were forced to work for the Malagasy in the vicinity of the concession. Also, Mr. de la Roche not only did not pay their taxes, as he had promised, but, it seems, still kept the money that these natives had given him for the payment of these taxes.

The administration, for once, had opened an investigation. But you will see…

Informed of the case, the agricultural Association of Mahanoro, of which Mr. de la Roche is probably a member, telegraphed the Governor-General to protest against the inappropriate police raid on the property of Mr. de la Roche and to ask for a sanction against the police chief, whose crime was to have discovered the French abuse committed to the detriment of the natives.

The Governor-General, in order not to "tell tales out of school" simply buried the scandal.

•
• •

The Council of war in Lille had sentenced to twenty years hard labor Von Scheven, a German officer, who, during the occupation, whipped the natives of Roncq.[50]

But why, in Indochina, a French gentleman who killed an Annamite with a revolver shot in the head; a French official who locked a Tonkinese in a dog cage, after having ferociously "cudgeled" him; the French entrepreneur who killed a Cochinchinese after binding his arms and having him bitten by his dog; a French engineer who "dropped" an Annamite with a hunting rifle; the French naval employee who killed a native gatekeeper by pushing him into a coal fire, etc., etc.; why are they not punished?

And why the young gentlemen from Algiers who, after having punched and kicked a small 13-year-old native and impaled him on pikes around "the tree of victory," had seen "imposed" a penalty of only eight days in prison – and that suspended?

And why did the N.C.O. who whipped Nahon, and the officer who murdered him go unpunished?

It was true that Annam and Algeria were conquered countries – as was Roncq; but the French of these countries were not the "Boches" and that which was criminal for the latter was an act of civilization when it was committed by the former. Finally the Annamite and Algerian were not men; they were the dirty "nhaquês" and dirty "wogs".[51] There was no justice for them.

The ironic Vigné d'Octon was not mistaken when he wrote: "Law and justice for the native? Come now! The stick, revolver, and rifle, that's all they deserve, these vermin!"

. . .

In the arms factories, woefully ill-equipped, penalties were imposed on the heads of the natives. There were fines ranging from 200 to 3,000 piasters.

Mr. Doumer was aware that the Annamese will never pay such sums; yet, he wanted to make money at any cost, and this clever man provided that *villages will be accountable*. (Article 4)

To condemn a whole village, you would certainly need, you would say, to establish its complicity.

Not at all, with Article 4, it was not necessary. Although responsible for an individual offense, the whole village would have been unable to prevent it.

This article 4 is diabolically clever because it is sufficient for farmers agents, paid to mete out the most offenses possible, to declare that the village did nothing to prevent such offense.

Title III determined the method of recording violations that farmers agents had the power to cite.

There is but one pitfall here. Most often these agents, who were illiterates, drew up irregular transcripts. It overcame this disadvantage by having the summonses drawn up by the customs agents of the capital, on the basis of reports prepared by the farmers agents.

•
• •

Indochina was a darling girl. She well deserved mother France. She had everything that the latter had: its government, its wages, its justice and also its little plot. We will talk about only the latest two.

Justice was represented by a lady with scales in one hand and sword in the other. As the distance between Indochina and France was great, so great that, arriving there, the scale lost its balance and the trays were melted and changed into opium pipes or official bottles of alcohol, the poor woman was left with nothing but the sword to strike. She struck even the innocent, and especially the innocent.

As for intrigue, that is another story.

We will not recall the famous rebellions of 1908 and 1916 thanks to which a good number of the French protected had been able to taste the benefits of civilization on the scaffold, in the prisons or in exile; these plots are already old and left no trace but in the memories of the natives.

Let us only speak about the most recent plot. While Metropolitan France had the resounding Bolshevist conspiracy, the gentlemen colonists of Indochina – like the frog in the fable[52] – also wanting a conspiracy for themselves, swelled up and finally had one.

Here is how they acquired it.

A French mandarin (résident of France, if you please), an Annamite sub-prefect and a native Mayor were charged with manufacturing this plot.

The executive trinity spread the rumor that the conspirators had concealed two hundred fifty bombs intended to blow up all over Tonkin.

However, on February 16, the Criminal Court of Hanoi recognized that not only the existence of a revolutionary organization with destructive gear was by no means established; but that the plot was just a provocative maneuver by government agents eager to curry administrative favor.

Do you think that after this judgment the incarcerated Annamites were released? No! It was necessary to maintain the prestige of the conquerors at all costs. To do this, instead of just decorating the clever contrivers of the case, we condemned, to 2 to 5 years in prison, 12 Annamese, mostly scholars, and on the door of the prison, we read – in French, of course – Liberty, Equality, Fraternity.

And the so-called native-loving newspapers hurried to sing the impartiality of this caricature of justice!

Listen preferably to the *Colonial Dispatch* which holds the championship for Annamiteophobia:

"French Justice has delivered its verdict. It is an acquittal for half of the accused and *light* sentences for the other half…Convicted were the scholars who had *celebrated the benefits of liberty* in bad occasional verse."

You see, it was a real crime for the Annamese to sing the blessings of liberty and they were tossed into prison for five years, just for that!

"We must," continued the same newspaper, "*welcome* the *highly impartial* verdict of our judges and our juries, etc."

And again, the *Colonial Dispatch* had reported, *with joy*, the highly impartial verdict of French Justice in the case of the famous Viuh-Yên conspiracy. The *Annamites of Paris*, like their distant countrymen, have demonstrated their trust in our judiciary and stated that they were right and that the case in question ended *to their complete satisfaction*. No, Mr. Pouvourville,[53] you jest a little too loudly.

⁂

The newspaper *France-Indochina* has reported the following fact:

"A few days ago, the House of Sauvage reported to the security service the disappearance of a large quantity of iron, about a ton, from his workshop. Upon receipt of the complaint, our officers immediately set to the task of finding the perpetrators of this theft, and we learned with pleasure that a European inspector of security helped by native security agents has just laid their hands on the thieves as well as on their accomplice.

"Mr. S…, manager of Sauvage's house, as well as the said Trâvan-Loc, apprentice mechanic, and Trânvan-Xa have been arrested and referred to the Public Prosecutor for theft and conspiracy…"

Did you notice the extreme delicacy of our colleague? When it concerns Mr. French Thief, who runs the Sauvage house, his name is suppressed, it is replaced with ellipses. The prestige of the superior race must be saved at all costs. But for common Annamite thieves, both their family name and first name is mentioned, and it is no more Mr. S…, these are the "named."

⁂

By the act of October 10, 1922, the government made a significant change in the colonial judiciary. We note, among other names, those of Messrs. Lucas and Wabrand.

It is worth recalling, briefly, the history of these two magistrates.

Mr. Lucas, who was Attorney General in French West Africa, is the same person whose name came up during recent Togo scandals. In a statement to the press, the Minister of Colonies was forced to declare that "the investigation also highlights that the participation of Mr. Lucas in the matter would impose THE HEAVIEST RESPONSIBILITIES on this judge."

It is probably in recognition of these heavy responsibilities that the President of the Court of Appeals of French Equatorial Africa is attacked.

As for Wabrand, his story is simpler and less known. In 1920, a French agent named Durgrie, of the trading house Peyrissac, went hunting in Kankan (Guinea). He shot a bird that fell into a river. A small native boy happened by. Durgrie grabbed him and threw him into the river, ordering him to go for the game. The water was deep, the waves strong. The child, not knowing how to swim, drowned. The parents of the victim lodged a complaint. Durgrie, summoned by the commander of the circle,[54] agreed to give one hundred francs to the bereaved family.

The unhappy parents refused this nefarious bargain. Angered, Mr. Commander took the side of his compatriot, the murderer, and threatened to put the parents in jail if they persisted in pursuing the assassin, and then he "classifies" the file.

However, an anonymous letter reported the fact to the Attorney General in Dakar. The senior magistrate sent the prosecutor Wabrand to investigate. Mr. Wabrand came to Kankan, spent the evening at the station master's and the next day at Mr. de Cousin de Lavallière's, deputy commander of the circle. He left the next day, without having even begun his investigation. This did not prevent Mr. Wabrand from concluding that the information was libelous. The Intercolonial Union reported the fact to the League of Human Rights (22 December 1921), but it is not interested, perhaps viewing the case as not sensational enough.

Since his visit to Kankan, Mr. Wabrand remains quietly at his post, receiving chickens and sacks of potatoes sent by his friend de Cousin de Lavallière, awaiting promotion. As you see, Mr. Wabrand deserved the … just reward that the government has granted him by appointing him Prosecutor in Dakar (?).

With the Darleses and the Beaudoins, the Wabrands and the Lucases, the superior civilization is in good hands and the fate of the indigenous settlements, too.

•
• •

The criminal court has just given thirteen months in prison to Fernand Esselin and the widow Gère, and ten months of the same penalty to George Cordier, for having possessed, transported and sold a kilo of "coco" or opium.

Very well. And that amounts to – by a simple calculation – 36 months in prison for 1 kilo of drugs!

It will, therefore, be necessary – if justice was equal for all, as they say – that the life of Mr. Sarraut, Governor-General of Indochina, be extremely long for so that he can serve the entire sentence; as it should be at least *one million three hundred fifty thousand* (1,350,000) months in prison *each year*, because every year he sells the Annamese over *one hundred fifty thousand* kilos of opium.

•
• •

Unable to get rid of the famous Dê-Tham,[55] not having succeeded in killing him, or doing away with him by poison or dynamite, the remains of his parents were dug up and thrown in a river.

After the protests in South-Annam, several scholars were sentenced to death or exile. Among others, Doctor Tran Quy Cap,[56] distinguished scholar, and revered throughout the world, was arrested at his post of professor and, without being interrogated, was beheaded twenty-four hours later. The Administration refused to return his body to his family.

In Haiduong, due to a disturbance that had no casualties, sixty-four heads were dropped without trial.

During the execution of the infantrymen in Hanoi, the Administration brought their fathers, mothers and their children by force to be present at this formal slaughter of beings who were dear to them. To prolong the feeling and "teach a lesson to the people" the governors redid what was done in the eighteenth century in England, when the heads of defeated Jacobites were planted on pikes in the streets of the City or on London Bridge. For weeks, on the main roads of Hanoi, we saw the heads of the victims of French repression grinning on bamboo pikes.

In 1908, burdened by ruinous expenses and exposed to innumerable harassments, the Annamites of the Center colony[57] demonstrated. Despite the entirely peaceful nature of these events, they were punished without mercy; there were hundreds of severed heads and mass deportation.

Everything is done to set the Annamite against his people and solicit betrayal.

Villages are declared responsible for disorders that occur in their territory. Any village that gives shelter to a patriot is doomed. To obtain information, the process, - always the same – is simple: the mayor and notables are questioned; he who is silent is executed on the spot. IN TWO WEEKS, A MILITIA INSPECTOR EXECUTED SEVENTY-FIVE NOTABLES!

For not a moment are patriots who fought in desperation distinguished from the scum of the cities. To destroy the resistance, no other way is found than to entrust the "pacification" to traitors who sold out our cause, and who make up these horrible columns of police in the Delta, in Binh-Thuan, in Nghe-Tinh, whose frightful image remains forever in the memory.

CHAPTER IX

Obscurantism[58]

To deceive public opinion in the metropolis[35] and quietly exploit the natives, the sharks of civilization add complete obscurantism to the stupefaction of Annamites by alcohol, and opium.

Thus, under the decree of 1898, the native press is subject to prior censorship.

This act says: "The circulation of newspapers and periodicals, in any language whatsoever, may be prohibited by a simple order of the Governor-General.

"The publication of newspapers in the Annamite language can not take place without authorization from the Governor-General. This authorization will be given only on condition that the text of articles for inclusion in these publications is submitted for approval to the Governor. This authorization is always revocable.

"Performance or delivery of songs, drawings or paintings contrary to the respect due to authority figures is a punishable offense."

You see here how dexterously colonial Anastasia[59] handles scissors!

By this means the Indochinese administration can smother all scandals and commit all abuses with impunity.

During certain municipal elections in Saigon,

the governor prohibited three managers of Annamite newspapers from publishing in their pages the copy of the order governing the municipal elections in the colony. These managers were candidates in these elections, and it was formally forbidden them to insert anything at all regarding their program. As no more than twenty Annamites have the right to assemble, the candidates were forced to see one by one the 3,000 voters who make up the electorate. At the same time, the Governor informed the other Annamite newspapers that censorship would be merciless for articles, snippets, titles or references relating to any colonial or municipal election. One of these papers, having translated into Annamite the text of the law punishing acts of corruption in the electoral process, saw said translation censored, while the unscrupulous Governor brought leaders to his office to urge them to vote, and make them vote for the candidate list that had his support!

This censorship is not limited to publications in the native language, but puts its despicable paws on private correspondence, and the French newspapers that refuse to sing the praises of our colonial Excellencies. The Post Office and the General Security Service of Cochinchina, directed by the son of Mr. Director Albert Sarraut, were ordered not to let pass, under any circumstances, the envelopes and letters, etc. addressed to the new Parisian newspaper, *The Pariah*, or anything that came from that newspaper.

For writing articles in *The Pariah* and other metropolitan newspapers denouncing abuses in his country by French administrators, a Malagasy, engaged during the war as a volunteer, and married to a French woman, has been banished and sentenced to five years in exile.

∴

In Indochina, the number of schools is grossly inadequate to meet the public wants. Every year, at the start of school, although parents knock on every door, begging for help, even offering to pay double the tuition, they are unable to squeeze in their children. And these children, by the thousands, are condemned to ignorance for lack of schools.

I remember a cousin of mine who, wishing to enter one of these education paradises, made multiple approaches, sent request after request to the Résident- Superior, the provincial Résident, the director of the National School and the head principal of the primary school. Of course, he received no response. One day, he screwed up his courage to deliver a written request to the French headmaster of a school where I had the privilege of being admitted some time ago. Our "headmaster", enraged at seeing such audacity, addressed him "Who allowed you to come here?" and he ripped the request to pieces in front of the whole dazed class.

The budget does not allow the government to build new schools; it is said. Not exactly. Of the 12 million piasters that constitute the budget of Cochinchina, 10 million find easy ways to rush into the pockets of officials.

On the other hand, fearing they are contaminated by Bolshevism, the colonial government does everything it can to prevent young Annamites from coming to study in France. Article 500 (bis) of the Decree of June 20, 1921, on public education in Indochina said:

"Any native, French subject or French-protected, who wants to go to Metropolitan France to continue his studies, *must get permission from the Governor-General.* The decision will be made after consulting the head of the local administration and the Director of Public Instruction.

"He must, before his departure, bring to the Directorate of Public Instruction, an academic passbook bearing his photograph and indicating his marital status, the address of his parents, schools previously attended, grants or scholarships from which he has benefitted, diplomas obtained, and the address of his correspondent in France. This passbook must be approved by the Governor-General.

"The files of natives who continue their studies in France are deposited with the Directorate of Public Instruction."

"Brutalize to rule," that is the method dear to the Governors of our colonies.

∴

L'Humanité has reported how, four years after the Just War, postal censorship is still strictly applied in Madagascar.

Madagascar has nothing to envy of Indochina.

We cited the case of *Pariah*.

97

Coincidentally, this new abuse of power coincided with the arrival in Saigon of the forger-administrator Baudouin, and his brilliant second, the chief of the police informers and son of Mr. Albert Sarraut.

On the other hand, the administration continued to stop and search private letters.

While natives were killed and robbed with impunity, they did not have even the most basic right, that of corresponding! This attack on freedom added a feather to the abhorrent policy of spying that existed in our colonies.

•
• •

The government of Indochina organized the sabotage of the *Pariah* newspaper, that of French West Africa prohibited the entry into the colony of newspapers published by black Americans; that of Tunisia expelled the Director of *Social Futures*. Mr. Lyautey drove out the director of *The Moroccan Wasp*. (The journalists were granted *one hour* to pack.)

•
• •

At the time of the opening of the fair in Hanoi and while Mr. Baudoin, Acting Governor-General of Indochina, toured the booths, police broke into one of them and seized the collections and albums of caricatures presented by *The Indochinese Argus*, whose criticism and satire were not to the taste of the powerful of the day.

Mr. Clementi, director of this newspaper, was arrested and put in jail.

CHAPTER X

Clericalism

During pacification, the Ministers of God did not remain inactive. Like bandits who lie in wait and panic people in order to loot after the fire, our missionaries took advantage of the disorganization of the country after the conquest to… serve the Lord. Some betrayed the secrets of the confessional and delivered the Annamite Patriots to the guillotine or execution post of the conquerors. Others spread throughout the country to solicit forced conversions. One such priest, "bare feet and legs, pants rolled up to his buttocks, belly girded with a belt full of cartridges, rifle on his shoulder and revolver in the small of his back, marched at the head of his flock, armed with spears, machetes and flintlocks. This is how he proselytized, at gunpoint, supported by troops which he led through the pagan villages reported to him as rebel."

After the expedition to Peking, Monsignor Favier, apostolic bishop and knight of the Legion of Honor, by himself pocketed a sum of 600,000 francs, the product of looting. "In front of the palace of Prince Ly," wrote an eyewitness, "comes a long convoy of carts and wagons, under the direction of

Bishop Favier, escorted by 300 to 400 Christians, as well as French soldiers and sailors. *They are movers in the interest of Heaven!...* The task completed, soldiers and sailors each received a check for 200 francs, drawn on the Congregation of Saint-Vincent de Paul." In an official deposition, we read this formal accusation: "The dikes of discipline are silently broken by this type of mass looting under the direction of Bishop Favier."

Naturally, Bishop Favier was not the only one to so evangelize. He had imitators. "At the lifting of the siege," wrote one, "the missionaries led the soldiers to the house of bankers they knew and in which were deposited gold bullion. They were accompanied by their pupils or by Chinese converts who performed the pious work of helping to rob their compatriots, providing the good Fathers with money for the Saints' uses."

It would take too long to tell here all the satanic acts committed by these worthy disciples of Mercy. We cite, in passing, the priest who held, pushed, beat, *bastinaded,* and tied a small native boy to a post at his curacy, then, with a revolver, threatened his boss, a European, who came to reclaim the small martyred one. Another sold an Annamite Catholic girl to a European for 300 francs. Another beat half to death a native seminarian. When the village of the outraged victim, while waiting for divine Justice, wanted to bring a complaint against the brute – pardon, I meant against the reverend father, - human justice warned the naïve plaintiffs in these terms: "Be careful my children! no stories, otherwise…" Bishop M… did he not say that French instruction is dangerous for Annamese: and Bishop P.., that God knew what he was doing by applying the cane to Annamites' r…umps?

If heaven existed, it would be too cramped to accommodate all these brave colonial apostles; and if the unfortunate crucified Christ returned to this world, he would be disgusted to see how his "faithful servants" observe holy poverty: The Catholic mission in Siam had 1/3rd of the country's cultivable land. That of Cochinchina, 1/5th. Of Tonkin ¼ in Hanoi alone, plus a small fortune of about 10 million francs. Needless to say, most of the property was acquired in shameful and unacknowledged ways.

"That which the settler does by using the State," wrote colonel B., "the missionary does despite the State. Beside the field of the planter is the domain of the church. Soon there will not be an available patch of land where the Annamites can settle, work and live, without resigning themselves to being a serf!"

Amen!!

.
. .

God is good and all-powerful. Supreme fabricator, he created a so-called superior race to lay on another race called lower, also created by Him. Therefore, any civilizing mission – whether for the Caribbean, Madagascar, Indochina, or Tahiti – always had a tow truck called the Evangelism mission. We know, for example, it was at the instigation of their colonial Eminences, supported by the wife of Napoleon III, that the Tonkin expedition was undertaken. And what had their Eminences done? They enjoyed the hospitality of the Annamese to remove military secrets, copy the plans, and communicate them to the expeditionary party. We did not know what this method was called in Latin, but in vulgar French, it was called espionage.

As the F. Garniers and the H. Rivières did not know the country and did not know the native language, the missionaries served as interpreters and guides. In these roles, the holy men did not fail to put Christian piety into practice. Some priest said to the soldiers: "Burn this village, it did not pay us taxes", or "Spare the other, it has submitted to Us." (Gl. B.) Us, that was the mission.

The colonial clergy was not only responsible for the colonial wars but their followers, the die-hards, scorned the "pre-mature" peace. In a report to the Department of the Navy, Admiral R. de Renouilly wrote: "I want to try to build relationships with the Annamite authorities to conclude a peace treaty, but we encountered great difficulties created by the missionaries… A treaty with the Annamites, as advantageous as it was, did not satisfy the desires of these Gentlemen; they aspired to the complete conquest of the country and the overthrow of the dynasty. Monsignor Pellegrin stated it repeatedly, and I have found the same ideas in Bishop Lefèvre."

Was it patriotism? No, because later, the Admiral said that "the church operating in Cochinchina sacrifices the interest of France to its private interests."

The following anecdote will illustrate this statement:

The King of Ham-Nghi left his capital occupied by the French. With his supporters, he besieged a village of defending Christians, including six missionaries. Alerted, a French general asked a priest to lend him junks to transport the troops to rescue the besieged. The priest refused, claiming that all junks were fishing at sea, and would return in three or four days. After making inquiries, the General gathered that the priest had deliberately sent away the junks expressly so the relief troops could not leave. Then he sent for the priest and told him: "If I do not have my junks in six hours, I will shoot you." The junks arrived, and the General asked the Reverend Father: "Why did you lie? – My General, if you had arrived after the massacre of the missionaries, we would have six more martyrs to be beatified."

Such was the evangelical actions our "Fathers" strove to do every day, and always in His name.

CHAPTER XI

The Martyrdom of Native Women

From what we have reported in the preceding pages, one can see in what manner the Annamite woman was "protected" by our civilizers. No place was immune from brutality. In town, in her house, in the market or the countryside, everywhere she was exposed to maltreatment by the director, the officer, constable, the customs agent and the stationmaster. It was not uncommon to hear about a European treating an Annamite woman like a *con-dhi* (prostitute) or like a *bouzou* (monkey). Even in the central market of Saigon, in the French quarter, they said, the European guards did not hesitate to beat the native women with blows from a black-jack or club to make them move along!

We could multiply these sad examples endlessly, but the facts already mentioned should suffice. We hoped to show our sisters in the Metropole the poverty and oppression suffered by the unfortunate Annamite woman. Let us see whether the native woman of other colonies – also under the protection of the mother-country – were better respected.

In Fedg-M'Zala (Algeria), a native was sentenced to one year in prison for theft. The convict escaped. A detachment commanded by a lieutenant was sent to encircle the douar.[60] After a painstaking search, the escapee was not found. So thirty-five women belonging to his family and his allies were rounded up. Among them were girls aged 12, 70-year-old grandmothers, pregnant women and still nursing mothers. Under the watchful eye of the Lieutenant and Administrator, each soldier grabbed a woman. The Notables and tribal chiefs were forced to attend this show. It was to impress them, they said. Afterward, they destroyed houses; livestock was removed, the raped women were stuffed into a room where they were guarded by their tormentors and where the same sadistic acts were repeated for over a month.

They said: "Colonialism is a robbery." We add rape and murder.

• •

Under the heading "Colonial Bandits", Victor Meric recounted to us the incredible cruelty of the colonial administrator who poured rubber into the sexual parts of a Negress. Afterwards, he made her carry a huge stone on her head, in the blazing sun, until death ensued.

Today, this sadistic officer pursues his exploits in another district.

Facts as odious were unfortunately not uncommon in what the good press calls "France Overseas."

In March 1922, an officer of Customs and Excise in Baria (Cochinchina) almost dispatched an Annamite salt carrier from this life with the excuse that she had disturbed his nap by being rowdy beneath the verandah of the house he occupied.

The best part was that this woman was threatened with being removed from the site where she worked if she made a complaint.

In April, another agent of Customs and Excise, who succeeded the first, made himself worthy of his predecessor by his brutality.

An old Annamite, also a salt carrier, had a discussion with her supervisor about a deduction from her salary. She complained to Customs. The latter, without further ado, administered to the carrier two strong blows. And while the old woman bent down to pick up her hat, the civilizer gave her a violent kick in the belly, which immediately caused a copious flow of blood.

      She fell, lifeless, but the associate of Mr. Sarraut, instead of picking her up, summoned the village chief and ordered him to take the injured person away. The Notable refused. Then the officer brought the husband of the victim, *who was blind* and ordered him to remove his wife.

      Want to bet that, like their colleague administrator in Africa, our two Customs and Excise agents in Cochinchina were not worried. They even got a promotion.

∴

      The small natives of Algiers are hungry. To have something to eat, kids six to seven years old are boot blacks or carry bread baskets to the market.

      The civilizing colonial government thinks these little outcasts earn too much. It requires each one of them to have a trading license and to pay a fee of 1 fr 50 to 2 francs per month.

      Workers of the mother country who protest against the unjust tax on salary, what do you think of this odious tax?

∴

Before the war, sugar, in Martinique, sold for 280 francs per ton; rum, 35 francs per hectoliter. (100 liters)

Today, the first sells for 3,000 francs and the second for 400 francs.

The boss thus made a profit of 1000%.

Before the war, the worker earned 3 francs per day. Today, he earns 3 fr. 75 to 4 francs per day.

Therefore, the wage increase barely reached 30%.

The cost of living has increased by at least 300%.

Add to this outrageous imbalance the reduced purchasing power of the franc and you get an idea of the wretchedness of the native worker.

In February 1923, following the refusal of the bosses to raise wages, the workers went on strike.

As everywhere, and in the colonies more than elsewhere, employers had little hesitation in spilling the worker's blood. Thus, during this strike, two young Martinican workers, one 18 and one 19, were brutally murdered.

The employers' ferocity spared neither children, nor women. Here was what the May 1923 issue of *The Pariah* reported:

"The bias of the authorities is clearly against the workers. All those who refused the job at the price offered by the bosses were reported, arrested, and searched by the police, who all showed the greatest malice toward the unfortunates."

Thus, the day before yesterday, two policemen went to Trinity Hospice to pick up a woman, Louise Lubin, who was wounded in both legs by bullets on the 9th of February, when Bassignac was shot. She was thrown in jail on the grounds that "through acts or threats, she would have undermined the freedom to work."

"But what is certain is that the poor woman could not walk, and the police wanted *to take her 32 kilometers away, by foot, to appear before Mr. Judge.*

"After she was arrested, it took five or six days before the doctor, who lived 32 kilometers away in Fort-de-France, visited her.

"Who gave the medical discharge, when this incarcerated mother of three children said she was not cured, that she remained disabled and could not walk?

"I mention this fact, alongside many others, also revolting, that recur around the colony.

"During the strike, on certain properties, the "lodged" employees were forced to work under the supervision of police and marines, as in the days of slavery.

∴

We read in a newspaper:

"In Constantine (Algeria), troops of meskines[61] walked around and begged. One of the unfortunates died near the El-Kantara bridge, her child in her arms.

"From Boghari to Djelfa, the trains were beset by old people, children, and women carrying babies in their arms, asking for charity.

"They had a skeletal appearance, covered with rags. They were prevented from approaching the stations."

.
. .

It is a painful irony that civilization – symbolized in its various forms, liberty, justice, etc..., by the gentle image of a woman and designed by a class of men who pride themselves on gallantry – subject its living emblem to the most despicable treatment and shamefully attack her morals, her modesty, and her life.

Colonial sadism was of an unbelievable frequency and cruelty, but we simply recalled here some facts that had been seen and reported by witnesses not suspected of bias and allowed our Western sisters to understand the value of the "civilizing mission" and the suffering of their sisters in the colonies.

"On the arrival of soldiers," said a colonial, "the population fled, the only ones remaining were two old people, a girl and a woman breastfeeding her new-born, holding hands with a little eight-year-old girl. The soldiers demanded money, liquor, and opium. And as nobody understood French, they became furious and stunned one of the grandfathers with a rifle butt. Then, for hours, two of them, already drunk on arrival, amused themselves by cooking the other old person over an open fire. The others, however, raped the girl's mother and her daughter in turn. Then, they laid the girl on her back, tied her up, gagged her, and one of them stuck his bayonet in her belly; he cut off a finger to steal a ring, and her head to grab the necklace.

"On the flat land of the old salt marsh, the three bodies were left: the daughter laid bare, the mother disemboweled, her left forearm stiffening up to the indifferent sky with a clenched fist, and the corpse of the old man, naked, as horrible as the others, disfigured by cooking, his fat that flowed into and coagulated with the belly skin, that was blistered, browned and golden like the skin of a roasted pig."

After taking Chomoi (Tonkin) in the evening, an officer of the African battalion saw a prisoner, living, without injury. In the morning, he saw him dead, burned, the fat flowing with blistered golden belly skin. Soldiers had spent the night grilling this unarmed person while others tortured a women.

A soldier forced an Annamite to indulge his dog. She refused, he killed her with a bayonet thrust into her stomach. The same witness recounted, "that on festival day, a boisterous soldier threw himself on an old Annamite, who he pierced with his bayonet for no reason."

A soldier, seeing a peaceful group of curious men and women enter his garden at ten o'clock in the morning, immediately fired on them with a a shotgun and killed two girls.

A customs officer who was denied entrance to the home of a native, set fire to the hut and broke the leg of the wife of the latter when, blinded by the smoke, the unfortunate woman fled with her children.

The unbridled sadism of conquerors knew no bounds. They pushed their cold cruelty as far as the delicacy of a bloodthirsty civilization allowed them to imagine.

The crushing taxes affect not only the land, animals, and men but their beneficial (!) effects also extended to the female population: "Indigenous paupers, loaded with chains, were used in cleaning the roads. They were guilty only of not being able to pay."

Of all the efforts that the civilizers had made to improve the Annamite race and to lead it to progress (?), it is necessary to mention *the forced sale of state alcohol*. It would take too long to enumerate here all the abuses arising from doling out democracy by the sale of poison.

We told how, to enrich the sharks of the monopoly, the criminal government of Indochina allowed its servants to force women and children to pay for alcohol they did not consume. To please the monopolizers, laws designed to punish smuggling were invented, placing on the head of the native an arsenal stocked with awful penalties. Customs agents were armed. They had the right to go on private property.

We were somewhat astonished, and that was something, when we saw arriving in Hanoi or Haiphong, long processions of *elderly, pregnant women, children tied to each other, two by two*, led by policemen, for offenses relating to customs payments.

But this was nothing compared to what happened in the provinces, particularly in Annam, where the Résident judge cages together young and old, men and women.

The same author then recounted the procession of parents, to the prison gate: "Elders, women, kids, all of them were dirty, ragged, hollow-cheeked, eyes burning with fever; and children were dragged, unable to keep up on their little legs. And all these exhausted people carried the most diverse objects: hats, clothes, cooked rice balls, food of all kinds, to be passed secretly to the accused, father, husband, or breadwinner, almost always the head of household."

All that had been said remains less than the truth. Never at any time, in any country, has violating all human rights been practiced with such cruel cynicism.

It is not only the continuous home visits; *but it is also the body searches that can be carried out anywhere and on natives of both sexes!* The Customs Agents enter native homes, *forcing women and girls to undress completely and, when they are in the costume of Truth, push their lustful fantasies as far as affixing the customs stamp on the body.*

Oh! French mothers, women, girls, what do you think, my sisters! And you, French sons, husbands and brothers? So, is this French "colonized" gallantry?

The enthusiasm of the Annamites for modern instruction scares the Administration of the Protectorate. That is why it closes municipal schools, transforming them into stables for gentlemen officers; it hunts students and cages teachers. A native teacher was arrested, brought to the province capital bare-headed, under the scorching sun, a pillory around her neck.

A chief warrant officer of artillery set fire to a house, on the pretext that the owner did not want to receive him at midnight.

A polygamous lieutenant threw a young Annamite girl to the ground and beat her to death with a rattan cane because she did not want to be his concubine.

Another officer had raped a girl in odiously sadistic ways. Brought before the Criminal Court, he was acquitted because the victim was an Annamite.

In every speech, in every respect, in all places where they have the opportunity to open their mouths and where there are bystanders to hear, our statesmen repeatedly assert that only the German is barbaric, imperialist, and militarist; while France, this peaceful France, humanitarian, republican and democratic, the France represented by them, is not imperialistic, or militaristic. Oh! Not at all! If these same statesmen send soldiers – children of workers and workers themselves – to massacre the workers of other countries, it is simply to teach them to live well.

· · ·

CHAPTER XII

The Awakening Slaves

I. IN INDOCHINA

In November 1922, due to a decrease in wages, 600 dyers in Cholon (Cochinchina), decided to stop working.

The employer offensive was unleashed throughout and everywhere the working class began to become aware of its power and value.

If these unfortunate native workers, usually very docile and easy to handle, uneducated and unorganized, had been pushed – by self-preservation, if one may say so – to join and fight against the ferocious demands of the employers, it was that their situation was much more miserable than could be imagined in Europe. This was the first time that such a movement took place in the colony. Mark this sign of the times, and do not forget that the duty of workers of the Metropolis was not only to give verbal solidarity to our class brothers there but to educate them, to teach them the spirit and the methods of organization.

II. IN DAHOMEY

French capitalism, worried about the awakening of the working class in Metropolitan France, sought to transplant its control to the colonies. It drew from there the raw materials for its factories and the human material for its counter-revolution. Bourgeois newspapers in Paris and the provinces regularly devoted entire pages to the Colonial Section. Generals and Parliamentarians gave lectures on the colonies. These virtuous scribblers and boasters could not find enough words to sing of our loyalty and the benefits of "their" civilization.

Sometimes these gentlemen pushed impudence to the point of opposing English colonial banditry, their… noble-mindedness; they described English policy as the "cruel method" or the "hard way" and argued that the French practice was full of justice and charity.

Just a glance is enough to evaluate how much this civilization was "beautiful and sweet."

In Dahomey, the already crushing taxes were increased for the natives. They plucked the young men from their homes and their lands as "defenders of civilization." Natives were prohibited from having guns to defend themselves against wild beasts that devastated whole communities. Education and sanitation were absent. In contrast, no means was neglected to submit the "protected" Dahomians to the abominable Indigenous Code, an institution that put man at the level of a beast and that dishonored the so-called civilized world. The natives, out of patience, rebelled. Then it was the bloody repression.

Strong measures were taken. Troops, machine guns, mortars, and warships were sent; a state of siege was proclaimed. People were arrested and imprisoned en masse. Here then was the sweetness of civilization!

III. IN SYRIA

The population of Syria was happy, very happy with the administration of General Gouraud, officials said. But the following facts proved otherwise:

In March 1922, Mustapha Kemal went to Messina. To receive him, the Moslems in Syria raised a triumphal arch decorated with black flags bearing the inscriptions: "Turkish-Arab brotherhood", "Do not forget your Syrian brothers!" "Deliver us!", etc. etc.

Mustapha Kemal's visit to Adana generated enthusiastic demonstrations. The irredentists of Antioch and Alexandretta[62] had paraded black flags in the streets of the city for two days uttering hostile shouts against the French Mandatory administration.

In reply to the manifesto of the irredentist delegation, Mustapha Kemal had said: "A home dating back many centuries can not remain in the hands of foreigners."

French colonialism had not changed its motto: "Divide and conquer." Thus the empire of Annam – the country inhabited by descendants of the same race, people with the same mores, the same history, the same traditions and speaking the same language – was divided into five parts. By hypocritically exploiting this division, the French hoped to cool the feelings of solidarity and brotherhood in the heart of

Annamese and compensated for them with antagonism of brother against brother. After having set one against the other, the same elements were artificially grouped into a "union," the Indochinese Union.

The same tactic can be seen in the new colonies. After having divided Syria into a "series of States", the French high commissioner in Beirut claimed to form a Syrian "Federation" from the "States" of Aleppo, Damascus and Alawites. A flag had been invented for this purpose. Like the flag of Annam, the French did not forget to graft onto this federal flag – at the top and near the flagpole – the "protective color." December 11, 1922, was the "solemn" day when this flag flew for the first time on the federal palace in Aleppo.

On this occasion, official speeches were made. Soubhi Barakat Bey, federal president, spoke of a "generous protector," of a "sincere guide," of "victorious leaders" and a lot of things. Mr. Robert de Caix, the acting High Commissioner, also talked a lot. Among other things, this official said that "independent Syria is not the first people whose cradle France has watched over," etc ... All these palavers, however, deceived no one. And at the Lausanne Conference, the Syria-Palestinian delegation, to defend the independence and unity of the true Syria - sent a protest letter, a letter that was published by our colleagues at *The Tribune of the East* and that we are pleased to reproduce here.

"Minister,

"When one tries to repair the breaches the Treaty of Sèvres (1920) has opened in the question of the Middle East, where the Arab people are located, one finds, unfortunately, that the voices of its representatives from the various districts most directly affected by the evils resulting from this treaty, proportional to the sacrifice they made (in the great war), still have no echo in this conference that was convened to establish a firm and lasting peace.

"And this is when the French authorities find it timely to crown solemnly the work of colonization undertaken four years ago by displaying the emblem of eternal slavery, the Tricolor, on the flag that has just been adopted by the so-called Syrian Confederation. It rejects, once again, the statements of the Allies, the commitments England made on their behalf vis-à-vis the Arabs, and even the promises of French statesmen ensuring independence to that unhappy country. Syria, which has clear title to prompt and complete independence, and that is not less worthy than any other country in the east or west, is deprived of a national flag. As a sign of the mandate, which camouflages annexation, it imposes three colors in its national flag.

"Mr. Speaker, we have always protested against the mandate, we have never recognized it, and we now strongly protest against the adoption of its symbol in our flag.

"Almost all the powers, even those that are no less great than France, did not adopt this method in humiliating their most backward colonies.

"The Covenant of the League of Nations specifies the provisional character of mandates (Article 22, Paragraph 4). On what basis, therefore, are French authorities empowered to have their colors adopted by a country they claim to lead to the independence already recognized by the aforementioned pact?

"Minister, consider our protest about this, and we reaffirm our very keen desire to assert our just claims to the conference.

"Sincerely, etc…

"For the head of the Syrian-Palestinian delegation,

"The Secretary general,

"Emir Chékib Arslan"

On the other hand, the inhabitants of Hama, many of whom were civil servants, lawyers, professors, journalists, and traders, addressed to the President of the Council of Ministers of France, a letter including the following key passages:

"We have the honor, Mr. Council President, to present our claims, as well as to protest against the reaction of the Council that we consider not in our interests or the country in general.

"1st Said Federal Council is not elected by the votes of the nation. Its members are not, in any way, the representatives of the nation, nor do they reflect its thinking.

"2nd Said Council is devoid of any power; it can not even address the vital issues concerning the country, constrained to dealing only with business submitted to it. Finally, its decisions are at the discretion of the High Commission, who can execute or reject them.

"3rd The very basis of that Council is skewed by the fact that each State has one vote despite the population inequality of the States. Add to this, the inexplicable oddity, that only unanimity counts on this Council, and that any differences end the debate. The question is then brought before the High Commissioner.

"4th Said Council, presented as a step on the path to unity, is the negation of unity and even the personality of the country. This Council, appointed to office, in no way reflects national thought; maybe it is even against this thought while in the eyes of the world it would be considered the interpreter of national aspirations and provide an argument against the nation itself.

....
....

"As for our wishes, we can formulate them in the following manner:

"a) Actual recognition of the independence and unity of Syria;

"b) Once the census currently underway is completed, we will conduct the election of a National Assembly by universal suffrage that will enact the constitution and determine the form of government of the country. This Assembly could be held toward the end of 1922, the date when the Federal Council will have convened.

"c) The formation of a government responsible to the Assembly with full legislative power.

"These are the real aspirations of the people of Hama; they are equally those of the majority of the Syrian people."

·
· ·

IV. THE RUSSIAN REVOLUTION AND THE COLONIAL PEOPLES

Capitalism is a leech with a suction cup applied to the proletariat of the Métropole and another one to the proletariat of the colonies. If you want to kill the beast; the two cups must be cut at the same time. If only one is cut, the other will continue to live, and the cut section will grow back.

The Russian Revolution has clearly understood this. That is why it did not merely make beautiful platonic speeches and vote humanitarian motions for the oppressed peoples, but it taught them how to fight. It helped them morally and materially, as Lenin wrote in his *Theses on Colonial Questions*. It called a congress in Baku, where twenty-one Eastern nations sent their delegates. The representatives of western workers' parties participated in the Congress. It was the first time in history that the proletariat of the conquerors and the conquered had extended a brotherly hand and together sought ways of effectively fighting capitalism, their common enemy.

After this historic Congress, despite external and internal difficulties that beset it, revolutionary Russia never hesitated to come to the aid of those people that already – by the example of its heroic and victorious revolution – had been roused from their lethargy. The first step was the creation of the University of the East.[63]

The university now has 1,025 students of which 151 are girls. Of these students, 895 are Communists. Their social status is the following: 547 peasants, 265 workers, and 210 intellectuals. There are, also, 75 ward pupils aged 10 to 16 years old.

150 teachers are responsible for giving courses in social sciences, mathematics, historical materialism, history of the labor movement, natural science, history of revolutions, and political economy, etc., etc. In the study halls, young people of sixty-two nationalities fraternally rub shoulders.

The university has ten large homes available to its students. It also has a cinema, which is available to the students for free on Thursday and Sunday, and leased to a contractor other days of the week. Two libraries, with 47,000 volumes, allow young revolutionaries to further their research and to feed their minds. Each nationality or "group" has its private library, with books and newspapers in their native language. Artfully decorated by the students, the reading room is filled with newspapers and journals.

The students themselves publish "a single copy" newspaper that is posted on a large panel at the exit of the reading room. Patients receive medical care in the hospital belonging to the university. A nursing home, in Crimea, is reserved for convalescents. The Soviets donated to the university two camps with new houses. Each has a farmyard where breeding can be studied. "We already have "30 cows and 50 pigs," said the agricultural secretary of the University, with ill-concealed pride. The 100 hectares of land allocated to these colonies are cultivated by students, who, while on vacation and after their work hours and exercise, go to help the peasants.

Let us say, in passing, that one of these colonies was owned by the Grand Duke. It is quite curious to see the red flag flying proudly on the turret decorated with the grand-ducal crown, and the small Korean or Armenian peasants chatting and playing irreverently in the great hall of "His Imperial Highness."

The students are fed, housed and clothed for free. Each receives five gold rubles per month as pocket money.

To give its residents the essentials of child care, the University patronizes a children's home and a model nursery, whose population is 60 pretty babies.

The University spends 516,000 gold rubles per year.

The sixty-two nationalities represented at the University form a "commune". The president and officials of the commune are elected every three months by universal suffrage. A student representative takes part in the economic and administrative management. All students must take a turn working in the kitchen, library, and club, etc. All "crimes" and disputes are judged by a court chosen and attended by all comrades. The commune meets once a week to discuss the international political and economic situation. From time to time meetings and recreational evenings are organized, where improvisational artists make you sample the art and literature of the most diverse remote areas.

The most characteristic fact of all, that illustrates the "barbarism" of the Bolsheviks, is not only do they deal with these "inferior" colonial brothers, but also they invite them to participate in the political life of Russia. In a Soviet election, the students who, in their country of origin, are the "subjects", the "protected", that is to say, they are not entitled to anything other than paying, who have no voice in the affairs of their country, and who are not allowed to talk politics, can participate in the popular vote and send their delegates to sit in the Soviets. My colonial brothers, who tire of begging in vain for naturalization, make the comparison between bourgeois democracy and workers democracy!

All these students have suffered and have seen suffering. All have lived under the "superior civilization" and under the exploitation and oppression of foreign capitalism. That is why all are enthusiastic and avid to learn. They are passionate and serious. They do not at all have the air of the boulevardier and young Orientals who haunt the Latin Quarters in Paris, Oxford or Berlin. One can say, without exaggeration, that the University houses under one roof the future of colonial peoples.

The near and far East, which runs from Syria to Korea – we speak only of the colonial and semi-colonial countries – has an area of more than 15 million square kilometers and a population of more than 1,200 million inhabitants. All these vast countries are now under the yoke of capitalist imperialism. And, despite their number, which should be their strength, these oppressed people have never seriously attempted to emancipate themselves, in that they have not understood the value of national and international solidarity. They did not have – like the peoples of Europe and America – intercontinental relations. They have in themselves a gigantic force they know nothing of! ~ The founding of the University of the East, by bringing together the young, active, intelligent people of colonial countries, marks a new era, and the University is undertaking a great work:

a) To teach to these future combatants the principle of class warfare, the principle of race warfare, on one hand, and the patriarchal customs on the other, which are unclear in their minds;

b) **To put the vanguard of workers in the colonies in close contact with the Western proletariat, to prepare the way for a close and effective cooperation, which alone will ensure the final victory of the international working class;**

c) To teach the colonial peoples – until now isolated from each other – to raise awareness and to unite – thus laying the basis for a future Eastern Federation, which will constitute one of the wings of the proletarian revolution;

d) To give to the proletariat of the countries whose bourgeoisie has colonies, the example of what they can and should do for their subjugated brothers.

.

V. PROLETARIANS AND PEASANTS IN THE COLONIES

The global carnage has opened the eyes of millions of proletarians and peasants of the colonies to their intolerable working conditions. A series of revolutionary explosions, powerful but not yet organized, marked the end of the World War. This irresistible, spontaneous force, that aspires to fight for a better future, was led and directed by the national indigenous bourgeoisie. Grown and strengthened during the war, the middle class no longer wanted to stay in the hothouses of imperialism and abandon to it the largest share of the value of "its workers and peasants." The struggle for national liberation, the slogan of the young colonial bourgeoisie, was greeted with enthusiasm and powerfully supported by the toiling masses of India, Egypt, Turkey, etc...

The International communist struggled tirelessly against the rapacious capitalists in all the countries of the world.

Could it hypocritically shy away from the national liberation struggle of the colonial and semi-colonial countries?

The Communist International had openly proclaimed its support and assistance for this fight and, true to its purpose, it continued to provide this support.

(Extract from the Manifesto of the Executive Committee of the Third International.)

VI. AN APPEAL BY THE PEASANT INTERNATIONAL TO THE FARM WORKERS OF THE COLONIES

The Peasant International, meeting in its first Congress, which took place recently in Moscow, marked its concern for the peasant workers of the colonies by sending the following appeal:

Farm workers of the colonies!

Farmers of the colonies, modern slaves who, by the millions, in the fields, savannas and forests of two continents, suffer under the double yoke of foreign capitalism and your native masters.

The Peasant International Conference, held for the first time in Moscow to prepare the fighting organization which was previously lacking for workers of the earth, calls upon your class consciousness and asks you to swell its ranks.

Even more than your brother peasants of the mother-countries, you have to work long hours, in misery, with the insecurity of joblessness.

You are often subjected to forced labor, to murderous portering and endless drudgery.

You are crushed by taxation.

Exploitative capitalism keeps you in darkness, oppresses you ideologically and decimates your race by the use of alcohol and opium.

The heinous Native Codes, imposed by capitalist imperialism, robs you of any individual freedom, of political and social rights, thus placing you on a lower rank than beasts of burden.

Not content to reduce you to misery and ruin, capitalism tears you from your homes and from your culture, to make you canon fodder and throw you into fratricidal wars against other natives or against the peasants and workers of the mother country.

Colonial outcasts!

Unite!

Organize!

Join your action to ours; fight together for our common emancipation!

Long live the emancipation of the natives of the colonies!

Long live the Worker's International!

Long live the International Peasant's Committee!

VII. THE TRADE UNION ORGANIZATION IN THE COLONIES

Extract from the minutes of the meeting held June 27, 1923 by the third session of the Central Committee of the Red Trade Unions International:

The Union Struggle in the Colonies

Contemporary imperialism is based on the exploitation of millions of workers in the colonial and semi-colonial countries. Also, the collapse of imperialism will not be complete and final until we have succeeded in rooting out the foundation of the imperial edifice. From this point of view, the organization of trade unions in the colonial countries acquires a particularly serious significance. Supporters of the Red Trade Union International have done almost nothing in this sense, not in Egypt, nor in Tunisia, nor in all countries that are under the boot of French imperialism. The liaison that exists between various groups of French colonial workers and French trade unions is only by chance. No systematic work is undertaken. However, it is obvious that before having won over the masses in the colonies, we will be powerless to undermine the imperialist organization. What is needed is a large propaganda campaign to create trade union organizations in the colonial countries and develop trade unions existing in an embryonic form. It is equally necessary that we overcome the distrust of workers of the colonies against representatives of the dominant races, showing them the actual class brotherhood between the workers of all nations and of all races. The organic binding of the colonial trade unions and those of the mother-country can only be the result of extensive work in the colonies.

Do not forget the workers of the colonies, help their organizations constantly struggle against the governments of the mother-countries that oppress the colonies. This is one of the most imperative duties of every revolutionary union, especially in the countries where the bourgeoisie enslaves and exploits the colonial and semi-colonial people.

MANIFESTO OF THE "INTERCOLONIAL UNION", ASSOCIATION OF NATIVES OF ALL THE COLONIES

"Colonial Brothers! In 1914, the public authorities, facing a terrible cataclysm, turned to you and asked you then to make your share of sacrifice to safeguard a homeland they said was yours, but which, until then, you had known only in the spirit of domination.

"To induce you, they did not fail to shine in your eyes the benefits that your collaboration would be worth. But the torment passed and, as before, you remained subject to the Native Codes, the special courts, deprived of rights which make for human dignity: freedom of association, the right of assembly, freedom of the press, the right of free movement even in your country; so much for the political side.

"From the economic point of view, you remain subject to a heavy and unpopular poll tax and to a portering tax, to the salt tax; to the poisoning and forced consumption of alcohol and opium as in Indo-china; to night guard duty, as in Algeria, to look after the property of the colonial sharks.

"For equal work, your efforts are paid less than your fellow Europeans.

"Finally, you were promised the earth.

"You now realize that it was all lies.

"What must be done to achieve your emancipation?

"Apply the formula of Karl Marx that tells you that your manumission can come only from your own efforts.

"It is to help you in this task that the *Intercolonial Union* was founded.

"It unites, with the agreement of Metropolitan friends sympathetic to our cause, all those from the colonies residing in France.

"*Means of Action*: To create this work of justice, the Intercolonial Union intends to put the problem before public opinion with the aid of the press and by speeches (conferences, meetings, using the platform of our deliberative assemblies by our friends who hold elective office) and finally by all the means in our power.

"*Oppressed brethren of the Metropolis!* Dupes of your bourgeoisie, you have been instruments of our conquest; by practicing this same Machiavellian politics, *your bourgeoisie now intends to use you to punish any hint of emancipation.*

"In opposition to Capitalism and Imperialism, our interests are the same; remember the words of Karl Marx:

"Workers of the world, unite!"

"*The Intercolonial Union*"

APPENDIX

To the Annamite Youth

Mr. Paul Doumer, ex-Governor General of Indochina, writes: "When France came to Indochina, the Annamite people were ripe for slavery." More than half a century has passed since then. Some great events have changed the world. Japan is ranked among the top world powers. China has had its revolution. Russia has chased out its tyrants; it became a workers republic. A fresh breeze of emancipation raises the oppressed people. Irish, Egyptian, Korean and Hindu, all the defeated of yesterday and the slaves of today are fighting heroically for their independence tomorrow. Only the Annamite remains what he was, ripe for slavery.

Hear this wretched prose, delivered by guest at a banquet for 200 guests, given in honor of the honorable Outrey, Valude and Company, and where, to sniff the odor of the socks of the bloc-nationalists the Annamite has not hesitated to pay 85 francs for some chow! "I am proud, says the Speaker, I am proud to express, on behalf of all, our feelings of deep respect, joy, and gratitude, for you, who, before our dazzled our eyes, assemble the government of the glorious French nation.

"There are no words nice enough to spell out exactly the meaning of our innermost thoughts, but, Gentlemen, be very certain of our faithful attachment, our sincere loyalty, and reverence for Guardian and Protective France, which considers us all its children, regardless of race and color.

"We have all seen for ourselves for how many benefits we are indebted to the High Administration and representatives of France in this country for the fair and farsighted application of liberal and benevolent laws."

At the funeral of Governor General Long, Mr. N…-K…-V…, doctor of legal sciences, doctor of political and economic sciences, attached to the Saigon Procuratorate, says that if all Indochina could express its voice, it is certain that this voice would rise sorrowfully to thank the Governor for everything he has done for the Annamite people. E. M. V. exclaiming:

"Those who, thanks to your liberal measures, take part today with the representatives of the protecting nation, in the growing prosperity of Indochina, thank you from the bottom of their hearts and venerate your memory. The economic question was your major concern. You wanted to give Indochina all the economic tools to make her a second France, the France of the Far-East, strong and powerful, and which will be a subsidiary of republican France.

"You were the heart and soul in your mission to civilize a people stopped on the road to progress by a combination of historical and climatic circumstances. You were the champion of progress and the apostle of civilization…"

For his part, Mr. Cao-van-Sen, engineer, president of the Association of Indochinese, said that Indochina mourns the untimely death of Mr. Long. And he ended his speech with these words:

"We sincerely mourn you, Mr. Governor-General, as you have been for all of us a benevolent leader and father."

From all this, I conclude that if indeed all the Annamese were also as groveling as these creatures of the Administration, it must be agreed that they have only the fate they deserve.

.
. .

There is no need for our youth to know that there are currently more than two thousand young Chinese in France plus fifty thousand more in Europe and America. Almost all are graduates, and all are student workers. We have seen for ourselves scholarship and other students, who, thanks to the generosity of the State or the capital of their family (one and the other are unfortunately unflagging forces) spend half their time at the academy…of billiards; half in other places of pleasure, and the rest; and it is rare that there is any rest, at the University or in School. But Chinese student-workers, they do not intend anything less than the *actual* increase of the economic condition of their country, and have a motto: "Live by the fruit of their own work, and learn on the job."

Here is how they do it: As soon as they arrive at their destination, everyone who has the same ability and wanting to learn the same trade, form themselves into groups to make representations to the bosses. Once admitted to the workshop or factory, they naturally begin as apprentices, and then as simple workers. It is very

painful for many who were raised in the luxury and softness of the family to do heavy and tiring work. If they were not equipped with a firm will and driven by a prodigious moral force, most of them would have wavered. But so far all have continued their work. Another obstacle that they were able to overcome through their powers of observation which is almost a gift for us Far-Easterners, and which our young neighbors know how to use for their benefit is language. If they do not understand or have difficulty understanding their employers, they observe carefully what is shown to them.

They do not earn much. With the little they earn, they must first be self-sufficient. They then make it a point of honor to refrain from asking for financial help from the government or their family. Finally, according to how much they make from their work, they pay a percentage to a mutual fund they have founded. This fund is made for two purposes: 1st to help the sick or unemployed students get a doctor's certificate for the first, and an employer's certification for the second; 2nd to give an allowance for one year to all those who have finished their studies, in order to enable them to take advanced courses.

In all the countries where they work, they found a magazine (always with contributions from student-workers). The magazine, in Chinese characters, keeps them abreast of what is happening in the homeland, and the major events of the day of both worlds, etc… In the journal, a forum is reserved for readers where they communicate information relevant to their learning, get to know the progress of each one, and give advice and encouragement. They work during the day; they study at night.

Coming with such tenacity, such desire, such spirit of solidarity, our "young uncles" will surely achieve their goal. Aided by a workers' army of 50,000 men endowed with an admirable courage and possessed of discipline and modern technique, China will soon gain its place among the industrial and commercial powers.

We have in Indochina everything that people could want: ports, mines, huge fields, vast forests; we have a skilled and hardworking labor force.

But we lack organization and organizers! This is why our industry and trade equals zero. So, what then do our young do? It is sad, very sad to say: They do nothing. Those who have no means dare not leave their village; those who have wallowed in their laziness; and even those who are abroad think only of satisfying the curiosity of their age.

Poor Indochina! You will die if your enfeebled youth does not revive.

Endnotes

1   A commission issued by the League of Nations (1919-46) authorizing a selected power to administer, control and develop a territory; the territory so allocated.

2   France considered Vietnam to be three separate colonies: Tonkin in the north, Annam in the middle and Cochinchina in the south. Combined with Laos and Cambodia, these countries constituted French Indochina.

3   Mission Civilatrice – the French fashioned their occupation of colonies as a civilizing mission.

4   general governors is a pun. The administrative head of Indochina was called the Governor-General.

5   Slang for German soldiers in World War I.

6   Ho Chi Minh had been away from Vietnam for thirteen years at this point.

7   French colonies were administered by a Governor-General in Saigon, a Résident-General for each of the colonies, and Résidents, or local governors, for each Province. Hence, the author's use of "our more or less general governors" above is a sarcastic play on words.

8   Batouala, the name of an African prince in a 1921 French novel of that title.

9   Charles Regismanset and Henri Hauser, French authors who wrote on colonial questions.

10   Cercle (Circle) was the smallest unit of political administration in French African colonies. Cercle consisted of several cantons each of which consisted of several villages.

11   poilu – literally means hairy. It was used to denote virility and was the informal term for the French infantryman during World War I.

12   nha quês – Used by the French as a pejorative term for the Vietnamese peasant.

13   On April 19, 1919, French crews of the battleships *Jean Bart* and *France*, sent to the Black Sea in support of intervention in the Russian civil war, mutinied.

14   Albert Sarraut was a member of the Radical Party who served in the French lower house, the Chamber of Deputies from 1902 – 1924 and then in the Senate from 1926 - 1940. He was twice Prime Minister. He was Governor-General of Indochina (1911 – 1914, 1916 – 1919) and then Minister for the Colonies from (1920 – 1924, 1932 – 1933) among other positions.

15   Messock is a town and commune in Cameroon.

16   The legendary sardine and good hostess refers to the mistaken myth that a sardine once blocked the Marseilles Harbor (it was a ship named the *Sartine*) along with a reference to the city's emblem, the basilica of Notre Dame de la Garde (Our Guarding Lady) that overlooks the harbor.

17   empyreumatic – tasting or smelling of burnt organic matter.

18   f… - ellipsis in the original, probably fuit (fuir) to flee, escape, run away, avoid or shun.

19   Louis Faget – farmer and French politician, advocate for agriculture and tobacco growers.

20   The reference to soap is a play on words. Laver la tête, literally meaning to wash the head (hair) idiomatically means to severely reprimand. It also implies cleaning this guy out of the place.

21   Indo-chinoiserie – Chinoiserie refers to decorations in the Chinese style, or a useless and complicated bauble, implying inscrutability. Indo-chinoiserie is a play on the word Indochina (Indochine).

22	Merci is the French word for thank you. When author writes m…erci, drawing out the first syllable as if he was about to say merde, he is implying the French word for shit (on you), because merci and merde have the same first syllable.

23	Pierre Loti is a French writer who had recently died. His novels take place in exotic foreign lands like Tahiti, Senegal, Japan and especially Turkey.

24	François Poulbot was a cartoonist famous for drawing children.

25	Raymond Poincaré, President and Prime Minister of France. Also, cousin of famed mathematician Henri Poincaré.

26	Another play on words. The author uses "taxer" which means either to tax or to accuse.

27	*Les Cahiers des Droits de L'Homme* – the monthly magazine of the French League for Human Rights and the Citizen.

28	bonne a tout faire – literally, maid who does everything; actually a helper who does menial tasks.

29   the author actually uses "fonctionnarisme" – the preponderance of officials in a state where, by their number, and their methods, they hinder or stifle individual or private activities. Coined by the writer Pierre Joseph Proudhon, a contemporary of Karl Marx. Proudhon coined the word "anarchist" and was the first one to use it.

30   Perhaps an allusion to the League of Nations awarding of mandates for colonies to   European victors.

31   1/1000 of a piaster

32   the author uses déquiller, which is a reference to tenpins, a game. Quille means both tenpins and keel, so the double or triple meaning, to unkeel them, to knock them over, a game with the double meaning of playing it from a boat.

33   The author uses "boy" meaning, houseboy or young domestic servant.

34   In 1916, there was a series of uprisings against French rule that resulted in the execution of 51 people.

35   *congai* – daughter in Vietnamese

36   passer à tabac – French slang for beating

37   light infantry

141

38 Le Dragon en bambou – the bamboo dragon.

39 Metropolitan France, as opposed to overseas France.

40 système débrouillard – meaning one who is resourceful at getting out of difficulties by any means necessary. Débrouillard means survivor.

41 Vietnam is a tropical country. The January normal low is 53 degrees Fahrenheit in the North.

42 caï-ao – coat or shirt, a garment with pockets.

43 name of a high ranking mandarin pagoda near Hanoi, meaning the big, large or mighty.

44 The Trans-Indochinois, the Trans-Indochina railroad was built by the French from the border with China to Saigon.

45 Rosette of the Legion of Honor, the highest French decoration.

46   This is a confused explanation of arbitrage. The 1920 loan of 55,900 francs was worth 5,466 piasters at   the rate of 10fr. 25. One year later, when the piaster had fallen to 6 fr., the loan was worth 9,325 piasters. The Résident then paid off the creditors with 5,466 piasters and pocketed the the 3,859 piaster   (or 23,154 fr.) difference.

47   drafted unpaid workers, forced laborers.

48   Khammés – in North Africa, an agricultural worker on rented land who receives 1/5th of the crop in payment for his or her labor with the land owner getting 80%.

49   The law of 1841 was social legislation dealing with child labor and civil jurisdiction.

50   Roncq is a small village in northeast France, three kilometers from the Belgian border.

51   nhaque and bicot (wogs) are racist slang terms for Arabs.

52   LaFontaine's fable of the frog that wanted to be as big as an Ox. The frog inflated itself so much in the attempt, that it exploded.

143

53	Georges-Albert Puyou de Pouvourville (1862 – 1939) was a French soldier who fought in China before holding several military and administrative positions in Tonkin. He became a Taoist and, as a writer, fashioned himself an expert on the oriental mind.

54	commandant du cercle – the lowest level European official in French colonies.

55	anti-French revolutionary (1860 – 1913).

56	Tran Quy Cap (1870 – 1908) was a poet and scholar active in the movement to restore Vietnamese sovereignty.

57	Annam – At one point, France considered Vietnam to be three colonies: Tonkin in the north, Annam in the center, and Cochinchina in the south.

58	Opposition to inquiry, enlightenment, or reform; *Oxford English Dictionary*.

59	Madame Anastasie was a cartoon character drawn by Andre Gill (1840-1885). She was an old woman carrying a huge pair of scissors with an owl overlooking her shoulder. She became the symbol of censorship.

60   douar/dowar – a small encampment of Arab tents grouped in a circle round a central enclosure for cattle. (Oxford English Dictionary)

61   derogatory term for Arab from nearby Ait el Meskine, Morocco.

62   Iskenderun, Turkey.

63   The Communist University of the Toilers of the East (KUTV) also known as Far East University or Stalin School, established April 21, 1921.

Printed in Great Britain
by Amazon